Gibran: Love Letters

❁

Other books on Kahlil Gibran

An Introduction to Kahlil Gibran
by Suheil Bushrui

A Poet and His Country: Gibran's Lebanon
by Said Abou Hamdeh, Suheil Bushrui,
John M. Munro and Marcus Smith

Gibran of Lebanon: New Papers
edited by Suheil Bushrui and Paul Gotch

Kahlil Gibran: Essays and Introductions
edited by Suheil Bushrui and John Munro

GIBRAN

LOVE LETTERS

The Love Letters of Kahlil Gibran to May Ziadah

Translated & edited by Suheil Bushrui & Salma H. al-Kuzbari

ONEWORLD
OXFORD

Gibran: Love Letters

Oneworld Publications
(Sales and Editorial)
185 Banbury Road
Oxford OX2 7AR
England

Oneworld Publications
(U.S. Marketing Office)
42 Broadway
Rockport, MA 01966
U.S.A.

A CIP record for this book is available
from the British Library

ISBN 1-85168-106-X

Printed and bound in Finland by WSOY

Acknowledgements

Like most scholarly works relying on many sources of information and assistance, this edition of letters represents a communal effort. Indeed, it would not have been possible without the approval, co-operation and hospitality of Dr Emile Ziadah, the owner of the letters, and of the Ziadah family.

Valuable suggestions about the text have been offered by Francis Warner, Dr Geoffrey Nash, Mr Charles Lewis, Miss Helen Simpson and Dr Albert Mutlak, but of course none of them is responsible for errors of any kind.

Finally, we owe a debt which cannot be properly described to Mr Mark Hellaby, who has given many hours of his time to labour both profound and menial which has contributed greatly to the making of the work.

SBB
SHK

Contents

May Ziadah

Introduction

I Known to English readers everywhere as the author of a long mystical poem called *The Prophet*, Gibran Khalil Gibran,[1] as he was originally known, is one of those rare figures who achieved eminence in both his native and his adopted languages. Born in 1883 in Bisharri, Lebanon, close to the famous Cedars, Gibran emigrated with his mother, half-brother and two sisters to the United States, settling first in Boston and later in New York, where he died in 1931.

Like many Lebanese, however, Gibran retained a warm affection for the mountainous region of his birth, and though he spent the greater part of his life in the United States, he never forgot that he was a Lebanese, drawing emotional and intellectual sustenance from the countryside and cultural traditions of his homeland. Therefore, though scholars have traced in his writings the influence of the German philosopher Nietzsche, French Symbolist poetry, and the English poet-painter William Blake, and in his paintings have acknowledged the inspiration of the French sculptor Auguste Rodin, one must also recognise the influence of the great mystical poets of the East and of the Lebanese countryside. He wrote in both English and Arabic, and though the topography of much of his characteristic verse is the timeless, insubstantial world of the mystic philosophers, it is almost as frequently the tangible rocks, stones and trees of the Lebanese landscape.

For Gibran, his homeland did not exist for him simply as a repository of picturesque rural images which he could use to add local colour to his writings. True, his senses responded to moonrise over Mount Sannin, the view of Byblos from the sea, the Cedars covered with snow, a shepherdess sitting beside a stream "that wound its way through rocks

1 Gibran's full name in Arabic was Gibran Khalil Gibran, the middle name being his father's. It is a convention among the Arabs to use the father's name after one's first name. He always signed his full name in his Arabic works, and this is the practice that has been followed in these letters. In his English writings, however, he dropped the first name and changed the correct spelling of "Khalil" into "Kahlil" – this at the instigation of his teacher of English at the Boston school he attended between 1895 and 1897.

like a silver thread", and he described such scenes in his writings. But his intellect was stimulated, also, by the historical and legendary associations of Lebanon, as revealed to him in a simple, white rock Phoenician temple, the towering columns of Ba'albeck and the massive ruins of the Crusader castle at Byblos. As Gibran expressed it: "Lebanon is a poetical expression and not the name of a mountain."

Impressed by the great technological achievements of America, and mindful of the material well-being of the majority of its citizens, Gibran viewed his adopted home from the vantage-point of his own cultural heritage and recognised that the picture was nonetheless incomplete. Consequently he sought to infuse some Eastern mysticism into Western materialism, believing that humanity was best served by a man capable of bestriding the two cultures and acknowledging the virtues of each.

Gibran's literary career can be divided into two phases, the first beginning in 1905, the date of the publication of his first Arabic work, and extending to 1918; the second beginning in 1918, the date of the publication of his first English work, and continuing to the time of his death in 1931. During the first phase, Gibran wrote exclusively in Arabic, but from 1918 onwards his work was mainly in English. His eight English books were either published or written between 1918 and 1931, two books appearing posthumously.

In his early years Gibran published five books in Arabic: *al-Musiqah* (1905), *'Ara'is al-Muruj* (1906), *al-Arwah al-Mutamarridah* (1908), *al-Ajniha'l-Mutakassirah* (1912), *Dam'ah wa'Ibtisamah* (1914). Between 1918 and 1931, during his second phase, he brought out three additional Arabic books: a mystical poem *al-Mawakib* (1919) and two collections of previously published work, *al-'Awasif* (1920) and *al-Badayi'wa 'l-Tarayif* (1923).

His Arabic writings in the first phase of his literary career are characterised by a strong sense of bitterness and disillusionment; Gibran's main purpose here is to reform society. He criticises, for example, injustice inflicted upon women; directs a scathing attack against ecclesiastical avarice and cupidity; and expresses his rebellion against the strictures of a bigoted and prejudiced society.

These early works, however, contain the basic themes of his later writings. As early as 1906, for example, he deals in "Dust of the Ages and the Eternal Fire" with the idea of reincarnation, an idea which he developed through the years into one of the strongest elements of his thought. Moreover, his belief in the healing power of Universal Love and in the Unity of Being are evident in *al-Ajniha'l-Mutakassirah* and *Dam'ah wa'Ibtisamah*.

In his Arabic works Gibran used the short narrative to express his ideas, but this was gradually replaced by the parable, the didactic essay, the aphorism, the allegory and the "prose epigram", all of which became distinctive features of his English works. But in both English and Arabic works Gibran's peculiar style is reminiscent of the Song of Solomon and the Psalms, with strong echoes of Isaiah and the parables of Jesus, the whole betraying the strong Biblical influence that permeates his work.

The second phase of Gibran's career saw the publication of *The Madman* (1918), *The Forerunner* (1920), *The Prophet* (1923), *Sand and Foam* (1926), *Jesus, the Son of Man* (1928), *The Earth Gods* (1931), *The Wanderer* (1932) and *The Garden of the Prophet* (1933). The last two were published posthumously; *The Garden of the Prophet*, left unfinished at Gibran's death, was completed by Barbara Young, who pieced it together from scattered manuscript materials and added many words of her own, utilising passages from Gibran's Arabic works such as "Nafsi Muhamalatun bi Athmariha" from *al-Badayi'wa'l Tarayif* (1923).

The Garden of the Prophet, which was supposed to be the second book of a trilogy beginning with *The Prophet* and ending with the unwritten but planned *The Death of the Prophet*, lacks Gibran's clarity of vision and sincerity. It is of doubtful literary value, though there are in it unmistakable echoes of Gibran's style and thought.

During this second phase, Gibran published his first and only collection of drawings. In 1919, *Twenty Drawings* appeared with an introduction by Alice Raphael; many consider that this book contains Gibran's finest art-work up to that date. He had been painting since 1905 and had exhibited his drawings and paintings before 1919, but this book stressed Gibran's mystical bent. It emphasised the direction he was to follow in his paintings and drawings as well as in his writings.

Gibran's message found ample expression in his English works, especially in *The Prophet*, which shows his view of life through the relation of man to man, and reflects his ideas on a variety of topics such as marriage, law, crime and punishment, freedom, generosity, religion, death, pain and pleasure. His message in *The Prophet* can be summarised as a passionate belief in the healing power of Universal Love and in the Unity of Being. According to the mystic tradition which Gibran followed, the key to all things is love; once that is possessed it frees one from greed, ambition, intellectual pride, blind obedience to custom, and awe of persons of higher social rank. This is also the theme of *The Earth Gods* and, to a certain extent, it influenced his portrait of Jesus in *Jesus, the Son of Man*; and it shaped the hero of his *Wanderer*, which crystallises Gibran's whole message of life, and captures the mood and atmosphere of his homeland, Lebanon, as well as his native mode of thought and phraseology.

II May Ziadah, the foremost woman writer in Arabic literature of the first three decades of this century, was the only child of a Lebanese father, Elias Zakhur Ziadah, and a Palestinian mother, Nuzha Khalil Mu'mar. Born on 11th February 1886 in Nazareth, Palestine, she was educated first at her birthplace and then for five years at the 'Aintourah Institute for Girls in Lebanon. In 1908 her father, a teacher by profession, seeking better prospects in Egypt transferred his home and family to Cairo, where he eventually became the Managing Director of the daily newspaper *al-Mahrousah*. For May Ziadah, then in her early twenties, life in Cairo, the centre of great literary activity at the time, stimulated her interest and encouraged her to publish in 1911 her first major literary work, *Fleurs de rêve*. Written in French and under the pseudonym of Isis Copia, this early work demonstrated the influence not only of her French education, but particularly that of Lamartine, the French writer and statesman, and pointed to the peculiar, exploratory, creative mind she possessed.

She was a regular contributor to *al-Mahrousah* and to the leading newspapers and periodicals of her age: *al-Ahram*, *al-Hilal*, *al-Muqattam*, *al-Muqtataf*, the French *Progrès Égyptien* and the English *Egyptian Mail* (for which she used another pseudonym—Re'fat Khalid). Her work as a reviewer of new literary works introduced her to Kahlil Gibran, whose influence on her thought and style can be seen everywhere in her works.

Although the two had only known each other through correspondence, a fascinating literary and love relationship came to exist between them: they seemed to have achieved a harmony and understanding rare even among people who are more intimately connected.

Her home in Cairo became the literary "salon" of the Egyptian capital, a meeting-place for all those without whom there would have been no modern Arabic literature. Her intelligent and lively mind matched by beauty and great charm attracted the attention of such leading figures of her time as Lutfi-al Sayyid, Yaqoub Sarrouf, Taha Hussein, Mustafa Sadek al-Rafi'i, Isma'il Sabri, Edgar Jallad and 'Abbas Mahmud al-'Aqqad. She became to many a muse and an inspirer, the influence of her personality and eloquence surpassing the influence of anything she has written.

May Ziadah's interest in creative writing was only equalled by her interest in the Women's Emancipation Movement, then at its height in Egypt, led by the Egyptian suffragette Huda Sha'rawi. The three years (1915–18) she spent as a student at the Egyptian National University (Cairo) brought her into closer contact with Huda Sha'rawi and confirmed her in the stand she took in support of the movement. This became her consuming passion to the end of her life and one to which the major portion of her work was dedicated.

Between 1927 and 1931 May Ziadah suffered the loss of four of the people dearest to her: her parents; Ya'coub Sarrouf, her staunch friend and ally; and Kahlil Gibran, the man she really loved. This series of bereavements affected her deeply, as her letters show:

> I have never suffered so much pain, I have not read in any book that it is within the power of a being to suffer what I have gone through . . .
>
> (Letter to Dr Joseph Ziadah)

Her condition worsened and she fell prey to long periods of depression which she tried desperately to overcome through her travels in France, England and Italy between 1932 and 1934. The last years tell a sad and tragic story of an unsuccessful suicide attempt, of her return to Lebanon to be under the observation of her relations, of her admission into al-'Asfouryyah, Lebanon's mental asylum, and of the horrifying experience of walking a tight-rope over the precipice of insanity. Rehabilitation came through the strength of her friends: Ameen Rihani came to her aid, encouraging her to return to her literary activities. On 22nd March 1938, May Ziadah proved, through a lecture entitled "The Message of the Writer to Arab Life", given at the American University of Beirut, that she was fully cured.

Much as she loved Lebanon, May Ziadah's heart was always in Cairo, where she decided to return early in 1939, and where she died two-and-a-half years later, lonely and friendless except for a handful of faithful admirers.

The bulk of her published work consists of essays, articles, reviews, translations, two biographical studies, a few poems, a journal and letters. Her place in twentieth-century Arabic literature has not yet been fully assessed, but it would be safe to say that her real achievement has been in the art of the essay. She is perhaps the most significant woman essayist in the Arabic literature of the first half of the twentieth century despite a style which now seems to suffer from a somewhat exaggerated emotional quality. At a time when few women expressed themselves in writing, it is remarkable to find a woman able to put before us with such honesty and force the deeper stirrings of her sex and generation. May Ziadah's life and art are inseparable; the suffering woman and the exploratory, creative mind are the same. Though an "artist" in the loose definition of her age, she was not a professional writer like Wali-u-Deen Yakin or 'Abbas Mahmud al-'Aqqad. She relied rather on spontaneity and freshness. Her restless life, her desire for experience, her rebellion against convention, were remarkable in the context of her environment and of her age, but in her last years through pain and suffering she was moving towards a spiritual humility and an insight into reality:

"Great pain is great purification."

III The love bond which brought together these two Lebanese writers living in different parts of the world, was one of the very rarest kind. There have been affairs which began with correspondence and then developed along the normal lines. More commonly, there have been relationships which were confined to correspondence after a traditional beginning. But

Gibran and May Ziadah knew one another solely from the letters they exchanged and from each other's work; they never met except in their imaginations and dreams, through the roaming of their spirits in search of eternal reality and of each other as kindred souls.

The unpublished love letters between Gibran and May Ziadah form a collection of unparalleled significance for Gibran scholars, following as it does on collections such as that of Anthony R. Ferris, whose *Kahlil Gibran: A Self-Portrait*[2] appeared in 1959, and Virginia Hilu's *Beloved Prophet: The Love Letters of Kahlil Gibran and Mary Haskell, and Her Private Journal*,[3] published in 1972. It sheds an entirely new light on Gibran's innermost feelings, never so frankly expressed as here. His letters to Mary Haskell were also full of passion, but although he loved her too, the relationship was of an entirely different nature. In Mary he found not only a surrogate mother but the financial and moral support he desperately needed as a writer and painter. Even in his most emotional outpourings to her, the underlying impression he gives is that of a grateful protégé trying to find a way of repaying the kindness and sympathy she bestowed on him in abundance. Ultimately theirs was a profound intellectual relationship upon which any closer intimacy would merely have intruded.

Gibran's relationship with May Ziadah differed in every respect from those he enjoyed with Mary Haskell and others. It is impossible to classify such a love, though it included spiritual and Platonic elements. Gibran and May were united in a sufi yearning and striving towards the "God Self". The "Blue Flame", which Gibran used as the symbol of God in man, also became the symbol of his eternal love for May. The two lovers joined in a spiritual procession towards the Blue Flame, the eternal flame of reality. This is what Gibran meant by his "longing" for May, a word that comes closer than any other to describing the nature of his feelings. For him love needed no words to express itself because it was a serene hymn heard through the silence of the night; indeed, the mist and the essence of all things.

The alienation and estrangement of Gibran, as a Lebanese émigré in

2 Heinemann, London.

3 Knopf, New York.

America, were both spiritual and physical. He longed both for the reunion of his spirit with the universal spirit, and for his place of birth from which he had been uprooted at the age of eleven. It is highly probable, however, that Gibran would have felt very much the same alienation had he remained in his own country, for in America he found himself a stranger not only among the native population but also among his own kin and fellow countrymen in exile. He saw himself as a wheel turning counter to all other wheels, an experience he described in *The Madman*, his first book in English. In this book, the only sane person able to remove his masks and look reality straight in the face is considered a madman by his fellows. Gibran may have confused his longing for the realm of the supreme reality with his homesickness for Lebanon; but in May he found in one person the incarnation of everything that his soul yearned after.

The correspondence between Gibran and May began about 1912 and continued right up to 1931, the year of Gibran's death. At first, their letters took the form of literary correspondence; exchanges of views, praise and criticism between two leading figures in Arab literary circles of the early twentieth century. May had apparently read other pieces by Gibran before she wrote her first letter to him on the publication of his Arabic novella *The Broken Wings* in 1912. In this first letter she praised his style, but expressed a lack of sympathy with the heroine, Selma, a married woman who meets her secret lover at prayer. While Gibran felt that man's only path to self-realisation lay in love, May was all too conscious of the inescapable position of Eastern women and the grip of social restrictions. Though she respected the freedom and individuality to which other women aspired, she could not disregard the silken bonds which tied her to her own society.

Gradually, however, after many exchanges, the relationship between the correspondents changed from mutual admiration to a firm friendship, but it fluctuated greatly before the final admission of love. Even then, May would invariably regret any tender words or revelations of the feelings in her heart; many a misunderstanding resulted from her diffidence, usually followed by a series of letters laden with symbolic expressions of emotion:

"My outpourings to you—what do they mean? I do not really know what I mean by all this. But I know that you are my beloved and that I revere love. I say this in the full knowledge that the least love is great. Poverty and hardship accompanied by love are far better than wealth without it. How do I dare to confess these thoughts to you? By doing so I lose them . . . nevertheless, I dare to do so. Thank God that I am writing all this down and not speaking it, because if you were here in the flesh now I would shrink back and keep away from you for a long while, and I would not allow you to see me again until you had forgotten my words.

I even blame myself for writing to you, for in writing I find myself taking too much freedom . . . and I am reminded of the words of the venerable men of the East: 'It is better that a young woman should neither read nor write.' At this point, Doubting Thomas appears before me! Does heredity have anything to do with this, or is it something more profound? What is it? Please tell me what it is. Tell me whether I am right or wrong, because I trust you, and by nature believe whatever you tell me! Whether I am right or wrong, my heart finds its way to you, and it is better that it should remain hovering around you for protection and tenderness to guard and cherish you.

The sun has sunk below the distant horizon, and out of the strange clouds, wondrous in shape and form, there has appeared a single brilliant star, Venus, the Goddess of Love. I wonder whether this star is also inhabited by a people like us, who love and are filled with longing? Might it not be possible that Venus is like me and has her own Gibran—a distant, beautiful presence who is in reality very near—and might not she be writing to him at this very moment with the twilight trembling at the edge of the horizon, knowing that darkness will follow the twilight, and light follow darkness; and that night will follow day, and day follow night, and that this will continue, time and again, before she sees her loved one? And so all the loneliness of the twilight creeps up on her, and all the solitude of night. Then she casts her pen aside, and she takes refuge from the blackness behind the shield of one name: Gibran."

(May's Letter to Gibran dated 15 January 1924)

But Gibran's letters never contained the usual terms of love or adoration. He wrote to her as if talking to himself about his childhood, his dreams and his longings for the East. The sketches and drawings on the sides of many of his letters to her show how much at ease he felt with her, and how near to him she was. Similarly, the invitation cards and paintings of famous artists he used to send her give a strong impression of how she lived with him day by day, despite the several thousand miles which separated them.

As well as being of unique literary interest, these letters clear up once and for all several biographical details which have hitherto been the subject of conjecture. Most important among these is the question of his date of birth, variously given by biographers as January or December 1883. Gibran explains in one of the letters how the confusion over his date of birth arose.

Gibran saw in May Ziadah the secret greatness of the East. To him she was Eastern womanhood personified. If he had met her and seen her "unveiled", perhaps some of her greatness and beauty would have evaporated; but, as things turned out, they never did meet, and she remained the dream and the reality for him to the end.

May must also remain an enigma to the reader. This collection of letters comprises only one half of the lovers' correspondence, those letters written by Gibran. Only half a dozen or so of May Ziadah's letters have ever been published at all, and those in Arabic. Her family does not wish to release the rest of them to public view. Perhaps the time will come when the entire correspondence is available to us; but until then, this collection, the first publication in English of the love letters of Gibran to May, is a valuable step forward.

IV The editors of these letters have attempted to translate them in such a way as to allow the luminous spirit of this unique relationship to shine through an alien language. Gibran's idiosyncratic key-words and terminology have been retained; a translation of complete accuracy was aimed at, but not one so literal as to be quaint. Certain difficulties are insurmountable because there are many Arabic terms which are simply incapable of being translated into English. Even so, the translation attempts to show the fullness of the Oriental spirit in an English idiom.

New York   2nd January 1914

[Dear Miss Ziadah,][1]

I have thought of many matters during the mute months that have passed without [my] receiving either an answer or a letter, but it never crossed my mind that you were "wicked". But now you have confessed the wickedness in your soul. It is only right and proper that I should believe you, because I believe and trust every word you say! Of course you take pride in saying "I am wicked", and you are justified in your pride because wickedness is indeed a force to rival goodness in its power and influence. However, permit me to inform you that, no matter how far you may go in your wickedness, you will never be half as wicked as I, for I am as wicked as the spectres that dwell in the caverns of Hell, nay, I am as wicked as the black spirit that guards the gates of Hell. And you will naturally believe this.

But until now I have been unable to understand what really prompted you to use "wickedness" as a weapon against me. Would you be so kind as to furnish me with an explanation? I have answered every letter you have been kind enough to send me, and I have also continued to probe the meaning of every utterance you have kindly whispered in my ear. Is there anything else I should have done? For have you not conjured up a sin so that you may demonstrate to me your power of exacting punishment? You have succeeded admirably, and I have come to believe in your "hypostasis",[2] that combines the swords of "Kali", the goddess of India, and the arrows of "Diana" worshipped by the Greeks.

Now that each of us has understood what wickedness there is in the other's soul, and its tendency to exact punishment, let us once again resume the dialogue which we began two years ago.

How are things with you and how is your health? Are you well and "enjoying vigour", as they say in Lebanon? Did you dislocate your other arm last summer, or did your mother keep you from riding so that you could return to Egypt with two sound arms? As for me, my health is very much like the ramblings of a drunkard: I spent summer and autumn travelling back and forth between the heights of the mountains and the shores of the sea, and returned to New York pale and thin to continue my work and struggle with my dreams—those strange dreams that elevate me to the very peak of the mountain and then bring me down to the depths of the valley.

I am glad you approve of *al-Founoon*,[3] the best periodical of its kind to appear in the Arab world. As for its proprietor, he is a sweet-natured youth, precise in his thoughts, and has to his credit some pleasant writings and original poems published under the pseudonym of "Aleef". What is admirable about this young man is that he has not only read everything the Europeans have written but absorbed it as well. As for our friend Ameen Rihani,[4] he has begun publishing a new and lengthy novel in *al-Founoon*. He has read me most of the chapters, and I find them quite beautiful. I have informed the proprietor of *al-Founoon* that I will be submitting on your behalf an article, so he is looking forward to it with pleasure.

I very much regret to say that I do not play any musical instrument, but I love music as much as I love life, and I am particularly keen on learning its principles and structure and deepening my knowledge of its history, its origins and its development. And if I survive I shall write a long essay on these aspects of Arabic and Persian compositions. I am equally fond of Western and Oriental music. Hardly a week goes by without my going once or twice to the Opera, although of all European music I prefer those pieces known as symphonies, sonatas and cantatas, because opera lacks the artistic simplicity which suits my nature and is tuned to my likes and dislikes. And now let me say how jealous I am of the *'aud* [oriental lute] you hold so close to you; and I beg you to say my name, together with my words of appreciation, when you play "Nahawand"[5] upon the strings of your *'aud*, for that is a melody I love and which I regard in terms similar to those opinions expressed by Carlyle on the Prophet Muhammad.[6]

Would you be kind enough to think of me when you stand before the majesty of the Sphinx? For when I visited Egypt I used to go there twice a week and spend long hours sitting on the golden sands with my eyes fixed on the pyramids and on the Sphinx. At that time I was a youth of eighteen with a soul that trembled before such manifestations of art, just as the reeds tremble before the storm. The Sphinx smiled on me and filled my heart with sweet sorrow and pangs of pleasure.

Like yourself I am an admirer of Dr Shumayyel,[7] one of the few men the Lebanon has produced who can bring about the new renaissance in the Near East, and I believe the East is in dire need of men like Dr Shumayyel to counteract the influences left in both Egypt and Syria by the "righteous and the sufis".

Have you read the French book by Khairallah Effendi Khairallah?[8] I have not seen it yet, but a friend informed me that the book includes a chapter on you and another on myself, so if you have two copies please send one of them to me and God will reward you. It is now midnight, so good night and may God protect you for me.

Yours sincerely,

Gibran Khalil Gibran

1 Before Gibran and May became more intimate in their correspondence he opened his letters with elaborate conventional forms of Arabic address which are virtually untranslatable into English. Here, for instance, he addresses her as "Hadrat al-adibah al-fadila" (literally "the distinguished and virtuous writer"). When "Dear Miss Ziadah" has been substituted for such forms of address it is placed between brackets.

2 Gibran uses this theological word ironically to mean "divine promptings" or May's special "divine law".

3 *Al-Founoon* was an Arab journal founded in New York in 1931 by Naseeb 'Arida (1887–1946) who was also one of the founders of *al-Rabita al-Qalamiah* in New York. His publications include *Benighted Spirits* (*al-'Arwah al-Ha'irah*), a collection of poems, and *Deek al-Jin al-Homsy*, a novel.

4 Ameen [al]-Rihani (1876–1940), a Lebanese author, born in Frayke in the north of Lebanon, who subsequently emigrated to New York. He wrote in both Arabic and English, and his most famous works include *Muluk al'Arab*, *Qalb al-'Iraq* and *Qalb Lubnan*. He was also a friend of both May and Gibran.

5 Arabic tune.

6 Thomas Carlyle (1795–1881), the philosopher and historian, never studied Arabic at Cambridge, but in one lecture on *On Heroes, Hero Worship and the Heroic in History* he glorifies the Prophet Mohammed's heroism.

7 Dr Shibli Shumayyel (1860–1917), a Lebanese physician and author. His works include commentaries on and explanations of old medical books. He was friend to May and one of her literary admirers.

8 Khairallah Khairallah (1822–1930), a Lebanese author who lived in Paris and was the director of the eastern branch of *Le Temps*, the French newspaper. He wrote a book in French entitled *Syria*.

New York 24th January 1919

Dear Miss Ziadah,

Peace be with your good and beautiful spirit. Today I received the issues of *al-Muqtattaf*[1] which you so kindly sent me, and I read your articles one after the other with great pleasure and immense admiration. I found in your articles a host of those tendencies and inclinations which for so long have surrounded my thought and followed my dreams; however there were also other theories and principles which I wish we could have discussed face to face. For if I were now in Cairo I would have begged you to permit me to visit you and discuss in detail [subjects such as] "the spirit of places", "mind and heart" and some aspects of Henri Bergson.[2] But Cairo is in the distant East and New York far away in the West, and there is no way we can have the discussion I hoped and wished for.

Your articles clearly show you to be supremely talented, well-read, and possessed of a refined taste in the selection and choice of your material, and in its organisation. They also clearly reflect your personal and private experiences, making your researches the best of their kind in the Arabic language, for I consider experience and personal conviction superior to all kinds of knowledge and all kinds of work.

However, I have a question which I hope you will let me ask you. The question is this: Might not the day perhaps come when your great talents would henceforth be dedicated to expressing the secrets of your inner Self, the particular experiences and the noble mysteries of that Self? For are not acts of creativity more enduring than the study of those who are creative? Don't you see that the creation of poetry or prose is better than a thesis on poets and poetry? As one of your admirers, I would rather read a poem of yours on the smile of the Sphinx, for example, than read an article by you on the history of Egyptian art and its development from age to age or from dynasty to dynasty. This is because by writing a poem on the smile of the Sphinx you offer me something personal, whereas by writing a thesis on the history of Egyptian art you direct me to the general and purely intellectual.

What I say, however, is not irreconcilable with your ability to demonstrate your personal and subjective experiences when writing on the history of Egyptian art. Nevertheless, I feel that art—which is the expression of what floats, moves and becomes an essence in one's *soul*—is more suited and conformable to your rare talents than research—which is the expression of what floats, moves and becomes an essence in *society*.

What I have just said is nothing but an appeal in the name of art. I appeal to you because I want to attract you to those enchanting fields where you will find Sappho, Elizabeth Browning,[3] Olive Schreiner[4] and your other sisters who have forged a ladder of gold and ivory between heaven and earth.

Please rest assured that you have my admiration, and be kind enough to accept my deepest respect. God protect you for me.

Yours sincerely,

Gibran Khalil Gibran

1 *Al-Muqtattaf*, one of the most famous Arabic journals, founded in 1876 by Faris Nimer, Shahin Makarious and the Lebanese author and scientist Dr Ya'coub Sarrouf (1853–1927). This journal introduced western sciences to Arab readers. It was transferred to Cairo in 1885 and ceased publication altogether in 1952.

2 Henri Bergson (1859–1941), the French philosopher and 1927 Nobel Prize Winner, who established the theory of spiritualism in opposition to the attacks of the schools of materialism.

3 Elizabeth Barrett Browning (1806–1861), the poetess. Robert Browning fell in love with her through her poems before the two met and eventually married.

4 Olive Schreiner (1855–1920), who used the pseudonym of Ralph Iron, was a British feminist writer on politics and women's emancipation.

New York 7th February 1919

My dear Miss May,

Your letter brought back to me "the memory of a thousand springs and a thousand autumns", and I found myself standing once more before those ghosts which disappeared and hid in silence as soon as the volcano erupted in Europe[1]—what a long and profound silence it has been!

Do you know, my friend, that I used to find solace, companionship and comfort in our much interrupted dialogue? And do you know that I used to tell myself: "There is, in the distant East, a maiden who is not like other maidens, who has entered the temple even before she was born, has stood in the Holiest of Holies, and has come to know the sublime secret guarded by the 'giants of the dawn'. She has since adopted my country as her country and has taken my people to be her people"? Do you know that I used to whisper this hymn in the ear of my imagination every time I received a letter from you? If you had but known, you would never have stopped writing to me—on the other hand, you may have known and that is why you stopped writing, a decision not altogether devoid of wisdom and good judgment.

As for the article on the Sphinx, Heaven knows I would not have asked for it had it not been for the relentless pressure of the proprietor of *al-Founoon*—God forgive him. It is against my nature to commission work from poets, especially from that small group which finds its inspiration only in what life itself suggests; and you belong to that group. Moreover I know that art makes demands, although demands may not be made of art; and that there is something in the very act of suggesting subjects which diminishes their intrinsic excellence as subjects for the artist. Had you then written saying: "I don't feel like writing an article on the Sphinx right now", I would have cheered: "Hurrah for May, she possesses a *bona fide* artistic temperament!" The gist of the matter is that I shall precede you in writing an article on the smile of the Sphinx, after which I shall write a poem on the smile of May, and if I had a picture of her smiling I would have done so today. But I must visit Egypt to see

May and her smile. And what might the poet say of a woman's smile? Hasn't Leonardo da Vinci had the last word on the subject with his "Mona Lisa"? Nevertheless, is there not in the smile of a Lebanese maiden a secret which no-one but a Lebanese is able to discern and describe? Or is it that a woman, be she Lebanese or Italian, smiles to hide the secrets of eternity behind that delicate veil formed by the lips?

And *The Madman*—what am I to say about *The Madman*?[2] You say that there is an element of "cruelty" in it, even an element of the "dark caverns", but I have never come across such a criticism before, although I have read a lot of what newspapers and magazines in America and England have said about this small book. What is curious is that most Western writers have approved of the two pieces called "My Friend" and "The Sleep-Walkers", singling them out for particular comment; but you, my friend, have found cruelty in them. What does it benefit a man if he gain the approval of the whole world and lose May's? The reason those Westerners are so happy with the madman and his dreams is that they are bored with their own dreams and have an innate weakness for the strange and the exotic, especially if it be dressed in Oriental garb. But as for those parables and prose poems published in *al-Founoon*, they were translated from the English original by a writer whose love for me is somewhat greater than his knowledge of the subtleties of the English tongue.

I have encircled in red ink the word "disgust", which occurred in your comment on *The Madman*; and I did this because I know that if you had taken my story "The Sleep-Walkers" and attributed the speeches of the mother and the daughter to the personifications of "Yesterday" and "Tomorrow", you would have replaced the word "disgust" with another—wouldn't you?

What am I to say about the caverns of my soul? Those caverns that frighten you so—I take refuge there when I grow weary of the ways of men, of their rankly blossoming fields and overgrown forests. I retreat into the caverns of my soul when I can find no other place to rest my head; and if some of those whom I love possessed the courage to enter into these caverns they would find nothing but a man on his knees saying his prayers.

I was pleased that the three illustrations in *The Madman* met with your approval, an indication that you possess a third [visionary] eye, in between your two eyes, for I have always known that behind your ears lie other hidden ears which can hear those very fine sounds that are so much like silence—those sounds, not created by lips and tongues but which emanate from behind tongues and lips, sounds of sweet loneliness, of pleasure and pain, and of longing for that unknown and distant world.

When I declare that "Those who understand us subjugate something in us", you ask whether I would like *anyone* to understand me. No! No! I want no human being to understand me if his understanding entails my spiritual enslavement. There are many people who imagine that they understand us because they find in our "exterior" behaviour something akin to what they have experienced but once in their lifetime. It is not enough [for them] to claim they know our secrets—the secrets which we within ourselves do not know—but they must number us and give us labels, and shelve us in one of the many compartments which comprise their thoughts and ideas, just as the chemist does with his bottles of medicine and powders. The writer who claims that you imitate me in some of your writing—isn't he one of those people who claim that they understand and know our secrets? It would be impossible for you to convince him that independence is the point all souls move towards, and that the oak and the willow do not grow in each other's shade.

I have reached this point in my letter without having said one word of what I meant to say when I began. Which one of us is capable of transforming the gentle mist into statues or sculptured form? But the Lebanese maiden who hears those sounds which are beyond sound shall discern both forms and spirits in the mist.

Peace be with your beautiful soul and your great and noble heart. God protect you.

Yours sincerely,

Gibran Khalil Gibran

1 He is referring to the First World War.

2 *The Madman* (1918) was the first of Gibran's books in English.

New York 10th May 1919

My dear Miss May,

I enclose the first copy of *The Processions*[1] that I received. You will find it a dream which is, as it were, half mist and half tangible in form. If you happen to like anything in it, then your approval will turn it into a graceful reality; if not, then it will revert in its entirety to mist.

A thousand greetings and salutations to your good self, and may God guard you and protect you.

Yours sincerely,

Gibran Khalil Gibran

1 *Al-Mawakib* (*The Processions*), one of Gibran's poems in which he followed the rules of rhyme and metre. He decorated the poem with symbolic paintings in which he expressed philosophical ideas. It was published in 1919, and May Ziadah wrote a critique of it for the Egyptian magazine *al-Hilal* (Vol. XXVII, pp. 874–9).

New York 11th June 1919

My dear Miss May,

I returned today from a long visit to the country to find your three letters and your beautiful piece published in *al-Mahrousah*.[1] I learnt from my servant that the letters—treasure of treasures—arrived all together four days ago. It seems the Egyptian Post Office has stopped delivering letters, just as it holds on to incoming mail.

I ignored all the other letters awaiting my return to my desk, in order to spend my day listening to your utterances, which alternate between sweetness and reprimand—I say reprimand because I found in your second letter some observations which, had I allowed them to, would have saddened my happy self. But how could I let myself dwell on a seeming cloud in an otherwise clear and starry sky? And how could I turn my eyes away from a blossoming tree to the merest shadow from one of her branches? And how could I object to a gentle stab from a perfumed hand full of precious stones?

Our dialogue, which we have rescued from five years of silence, will never turn to recrimination or blame, for I accept all you say in the belief that it would not be becoming to add even an inch to the seven thousand miles which separate us; indeed, we must try to shorten that distance with what God has instilled in us in the way of leaning towards that which is beautiful, longing for that which is the source, and thirsting for that which is eternal. In these days, my friend, there is quite enough in the way of pain, confusion, difficulties and obstacles. And in my opinion an idea that can stand before the absolute and the elemental is immune to the effects of a word or phrase in a book or an observation made in a letter. So let us put aside our differences—most of which are verbal—let us deposit them in a golden coffer and throw it into a sea of smiles.

How sweet your letters are, May, and how delightful. They are like a river of nectar which flows down from the mountain-top and sings its way into the valley of my dreams. Indeed, they are like Orpheus' lute, which attracts things that are far away and advances things that are near, and by means of its enchanted reverberations turns stones into glowing torches and boughs into agitated wings. The day when just one of your letters arrives is equal to the peak of the mountain for me—so what am I to say of a day when three letters all come at once? That is indeed a day on which I forsake the well-trodden paths of time to roam the streets of "Iram, City of Lofty Pillars".[2]

How am I to answer your questions? And how am I to continue our dialogue when my heart contains something which cannot flow in ink? Yet we must continue the dialogue. But you do understand what remains unsaid.

You say in your first letter that "if I were in New York I would visit your studio". Haven't you visited my studio?

My studio is my temple, my friend, my museum, my heaven and my hell. It is a forest in which life calls out to life, and a desert with me standing in its midst and seeing nothing but a sea of sand and a sea of ether. My studio is a house without walls or roof, my friend. In this studio of mine there are many things which I keep and cherish. I am [particularly] fond of the antique objects. In the corners of this studio is a small collection of rare and precious things from past ages, such as statues and slates from Egypt, Greece and Rome; Phoenician glass; Persian pottery; ancient books and French and Italian paintings; and musical instruments which speak even in their silence. But some day I must acquire a Chaldean black-stone statue. For I have a special fondness for everything Chaldean; the myths of the Chaldeans, their poetry, their prayers, their geometry, even the minutest relics time has left behind of their art and crafts, all these stir distant and mysterious memories within me, transporting me to days gone by and allowing me to see the past through the window of the future. I love antique objects, and they appeal to me because they are the fruit of human thought marching in a procession of a thousand stamping feet out of the darkness and into the light—that eternal thought which plunges deep down to the bottom of the sea only to rise up to the Milky Way.

As for your statement "How happy you are, you who find contentment in your art"—this made me ponder for a long time. No, May, I am neither happy nor content. In me there is something which can never be content, but does not resemble covetousness; something which can never know happiness but does not resemble misery. In my depths there is a continual throb and an incessant pain, and I desire to change neither the one nor the other—a man in such a plight cannot know happiness or recognise contentment, but he does not complain because in complaining there is a certain comfort and transcendence.

Are you happy and content with your great talents? Tell me, May, are you happy and content? I can almost hear you whispering: "No, I am neither happy nor content." Contentment is satisfaction, and satisfaction is limited—whereas you are not limited. As for happiness, this comes when one is drunk with the wine of life; but he whose cup is seven thousand leagues deep and seven thousand leagues wide can never know happiness unless life in its entirety be poured into his cup. Is not your own cup, May, one of a thousand-and-one leagues?

What am I to say of "my state of mind"? My life a year or two ago was not empty of tranquillity and peace, but today tranquillity has been transformed into noise and peace into strife. People devour my days and nights, and inundate my dreams with their ambitions and inclinations; many a time I have escaped from this city, which is drifting towards a far-off destination, so that I might rid my Self of people—and of the ghosts of my [acquired] self. The Americans are a mighty people, indefatigable, persistent, unflagging, sleepless and dreamless. If they hate someone, they kill him with indifference; if they love someone, they smother him with kindness. He who wishes to live in New York should keep a sharp sword by him, but in a sheath full of honey; a sword to punish those who like to kill time, and honey to gratify those who are hungry.

The day will come when I shall escape to the East. My longing for my homeland almost destroys me, and were it not for the cage around me, the bars of which I forged with my own hands, I would board the first ship bound for the East. But what man is capable of forsaking the house built from stones which he has spent a lifetime hewing and positioning—even if that house were his prison because he was neither able nor willing to forsake it for a single day.

Forgive me, dear friend, for troubling you with this talk of myself, and for complaining about matters in which we should be struggling for achievement rather than complaining.

Your approval of *The Processions* has endeared that poem to me; as for your declaration that you intend memorising its verses, I am so beholden to you that I humbly bow my head. However, I am inclined to feel that your retentive faculties are worthy of memorising poems far more exalted, eloquent and noble than anything I have written in *The Processions* or elsewhere or am writing now. As for what you say about the drawings in the book: "You artists express these wonders by means of the powers entrusted you by the kings of the firmament, and we the audience are helpless when we confront such wonders, for we possess nothing with which to understand them; so you are misjudged owing to our ignorance, in consequence of which we are miserable and we are the losers."

This is the kind of talk which I do not accept, and I beg to rebel against it (and how often I have rebelled). You are one of us, May, you really are among the sons and daughters of art like the rose in the midst of the rose-leaves. Your article in *al-Mahrousah* contains passages about the drawings in *The Madman* which are proof enough of your deep artistic perception, showing you to have a very special point of view and a critical faculty that allows you to observe that which very few people can. It would be no exaggeration for me to say: "You are the first Eastern girl to walk in the forest inhabited by the Pleiades,[3] with sureness of foot, head erect, and smiling as if it were her own father's house." Tell me, how did you come by all you know, from what have you derived the treasures hidden within yourself, and in which age did your soul live before it came to Lebanon? In genius there lies a mystery far more profound than the mystery of life itself.

You would like to know what Westerners say about me. A thousand thanks for your enthusiasm and patriotism. They have said a great deal, they have exaggerated in what they said, and they have gone to extremes in expressing their opinions, thinking me a camel rather than a rabbit. And God knows, my dear friend, that I have not read any such eulogy of myself without its etching itself painfully on my heart. Approbation is a form of responsibility foisted on us by others, causing us to become aware of our own weakness. However, we must continue to move forward though the heavy burden bends our backs, and we must draw strength from our weakness.

I am sending you some magazine and newspaper clippings under separate cover, and you will see that Westerners have become bored with the ghosts of their souls and have grown weary of themselves—so they latch onto the exotic and the unfamiliar, especially things Oriental. The people of Athens were like this after the eclipse of their Golden Age. Over a month ago I sent a collection of press cuttings relating to *The Madman* to Mr Emil Zaydan[4]—he, of course, is one of your friends.

I praise and thank God that the crisis is over at your end. I used to read the news about the demonstrations and would imagine your alarm and agitation, which in turn made me alarmed and agitated. In either case I would recite the words of Shakespeare to myself:

. . .do not fear our person,
There's such divinity doth hedge a king,
That treason can but peep to what it would,
Acts little of his will.[5]

You, May, are among those who are protected; and within your Self is an angel who God guards from all evil.

You also ask whether you have any friends in this part of the world.

By this life and what it contains of wounding sweetness and divine bitterness, you *do* have a friend in this part of the world. He is resolved to defend you, he wishes you well and will see that no harm comes to you. A friend who is far away is sometimes much nearer than one who is at hand. Is not the mountain far more awe-inspiring and more clearly visible to one passing through the valley than to those who inhabit the mountain?

The night has drawn its veil over the studio, and I can no longer see what my hand is writing. A thousand greetings to you and a thousand salutations, and may God protect and guard you always.

Your sincere friend,

Gibran Khalil Gibran

1 *Al-Mahrousah*, an Egyptian newspaper founded in 1881. May's father, Elias Ziadah, was one of its editors in 1908, and then became the owner, with May as one of his editors. After his death in 1929, she became owner and editor-in-chief.

2 "Iram, City of Lofty Pillars" was mentioned in the Qur'an. It was the country inhabited by the tribe of 'Add, and was built on pillars. Gibran borrowed the name for a sufi play which he wrote and had published in 1921.

3 A reference to the Pleiades of Greek mythology, the seven daughters of Atlas, known by various names in ancient times, who supervised literature, arts and sciences.

4 Emil Zaydan, who became editor-in-chief of the journal *al-Hilal* in 1914, which was founded by his father, George Zaydan.

5 *Hamlet*, Act IV, Scene 5, ll.123–6.

New York 11th June 1919

An envelope postmarked 11–6–19 contained some newspaper clippings—reviews by American critics of The Madman*—on one of which Gibran had scrawled the following.*

The Madman has now been translated into French, Italian and Russian, and parts of it into other languages. The French translation will be appearing soon, and I will send you a copy in due course.

THE MADMAN. By Kahlil Gibran. Knopf; $1.25.

It is not strange that Rodin should have hoped much of this Arabian poet. For in those parables and poems which Gibran has given us in English he curiously seems to express what Rodin did with marble and clay. Both sculptor and poet show an imagination which goes to the mountains and the elements for strength, a desire to give human things a universal quality, a mellow irony, and a love of truth which is not afraid of platitudes. Rodin compared Gibran to William Blake. But the parables collected in The Madman are more reminiscent of Zarathustra's maskings and unmaskings, of the long rising rhythms of Tagore. The English language never seems a fit medium for work of this nature. It is too angular, too resisting to hold the meanings which Oriental literature crowds as thickly and dazzingly as jewels on an encrusted sword-hilt. It would be interesting at least to see what a French translator would make of these poems:

For what is there can quench a madman's thirst but his own blood? I was dumb—and I asked wounds of you for mouths. I was imprisoned in your days and nights—and I sought a door into larger days and nights.

And now I go—as others already crucified have gone. And think not we are weary of crucifixion. For we must be crucified by larger and yet larger men, between greater earths and greater heavens.

New York 25th July 1919

My dear Miss May,

You have been in my mind ever since I last wrote to you. I have spent long hours thinking of you, talking to you, endeavouring to discover your secrets, trying to unravel your mysteries. Even so, it is still surprising to me that I should have felt the presence of your ethereal [incorporeal] Self in my study, watching the moves I make, conversing and arguing with me, voicing opinions on what I do.

You will naturally be surprised to hear me talk like this; I myself find it strange that I should feel this urge and this necessity to write to you. I wish it were possible for me to comprehend the hidden secret behind this necessity, this urgent need.

You once said that "there is always a dialectic between minds and an interplay of thoughts, [both of] which lie beyond sensory awareness; and no-one can ever entirely erase that interplay and dialectic from the minds and thoughts of those who belong to the same native land".

In this beautiful passage resides a fundamental truth, once clear to me through a kind of mental empathy, but now clear to me through personal experience. I have recently established a bond, abstract, delicate, firm, strange and unlike all other bonds in its nature and characteristics, a bond which cannot be compared to the natural familial bonds, a bond which, indeed, is far more steadfast, firm and permanent even than moral bonds.

Not a single one of the threads which form this bond was woven by the days and nights which measure time and intersperse the distance that separates the cradle from the grave. Not a single one of those threads was woven by past interests or future aspirations—for this bond has existed between two people who were brought together by neither the past nor the present, and who may not be united by the future, either.

In such a bond, May, in such a private emotion, in such a secret understanding, there exist dreams more exotic and more unfathomable than anything that surges in the human breast; dreams within dreams within dreams.

Such an understanding, May, is a deep and silent song which is heard in the stillness of the night; it transports us beyond the realms of day, beyond the realms of night, beyond time, beyond eternity.

Such an emotion, May, involves sharp pangs that will never disappear, but which are dear to us, and which we would not exchange, even if we had the chance, for any amount of glory or pleasure, known or imagined.

The above is an attempt to communicate to you that which cannot be communicated to you by anyone other than him who shares in all that is within you. If, therefore, I have fathomed a secret with which you yourself are not unacquainted, then I am one of those to whom Life has granted her gifts and permitted to stand before the White Throne; but if I have fathomed that which is peculiar to me and in myself alone, then let the fire consume this letter.

I implore you, my friend, to write to me; and I implore you to write in that free, detached, winged spirit that soars far above the ways of mankind. You and I know a great deal about mankind, about the interests that bring people together, and about the facts that drive them apart.

May we not withdraw awhile from those well-worn paths, and may we not pause for a time to gaze into the realms which lie beyond night, beyond day, beyond time, beyond eternity?

May God keep you, May, and may he protect you always.

Your true friend,

Gibran Khalil Gibran

New York 26th July 1919

An envelope postmarked 26–7–19 contained a newspaper clipping—see below—and part of Alice Raphael's introduction to Gibran's first art book, Twenty Drawings, *with the following note in Gibran's handwriting.*

This book will be published in early autumn, and I will send you the first copy that I receive.

TWENTY DRAWINGS
By
KAHLIL GIBRAN
Author of "The Madman"
With an Introductory Essay by
ALICE RAPHAEL

Quarto, half cloth, French board sides, $3.00 *net.*

سيصدر هذا الكتاب في اوائل
الخريف وسأبعث اليك بأول
نسخة تبلغ يدي

KAHLIL GIBRAN'S poetry is known not only to the millions who speak Arabic, but since the publication of *The Madman,* his first work in English, to Europe and America as well. His art has much of the quality of his poetry. Auguste Rodin, his friend, said of him: "I know of no one else in whom drawing and poetry are so linked together as to make him a new Blake."

These pictures represent the human form in attitudes expressing the eternal verities. There is the "Erdgeist"—the spirit of creation; the Transfiguration, expressing the suffering of mankind; there are delightful, delicate pictures of the Centaurs—who but Gibran could portray a *delicate* Centaur?—in their legendary battles, expressing the struggle of man against his brute nature. Of the twenty drawings one is in full color, the rest in wash with very faint pencil lining. The introductory appreciation is informing and complete.

The whole is a representative collection of the best work of one of the most remarkable figures of the day—a man who has brought the mysticism of the Near East to America and has chosen to throw in his lot with the artists of the occident in an endeavor to fuse new bonds of interest between the old world and the new.

New York 9th November 1919

My dear Miss May,

You are angry and displeased with me, and you have every right to be. I, for my part, can do nothing but resign myself to your will. Can you not forget whatever it is that I have done wrong, I who am so far removed from the world of weighing and measuring? Will you not deposit in the [worldly] "golden coffer" that which is unworthy to be kept in the "ethereal coffer"?

Someone who is absent cannot possess the first-hand knowledge of someone who is present; and it is unfair to consider that a crime. For there is no crime without knowledge or awareness. I do not wish inadvertently to pour molten lead or boiling water on the hands of those who possess full knowledge, for I know that any crime is in itself a punishment for the criminal, and that the tragedy in most people's lives is inherent in the work assigned to them.

I have found comfort and solace in that translucent element before which all distances, barriers and obstacles vanish away. And the lonely find solace and comfort in nothing but that element, appealing to and seeking the aid of no other. For you—you, who so often dwell in the world of inner meaning—know that the translucent element in us is aloof and remote from all that we do, even from the most eloquent of verbal expressions and the noblest of artistic aspirations. For even if it were akin to the poetic in us, it could not of itself create lyrics, nor could it give form or colour to its mysteries. Every human being is capable of counterfeit when it comes to his likes and dislikes, and of juggling with his ambitions and bartering his thoughts; but no man on earth is capable of counterfeit with regard to his loneliness, or of juggling with or bartering his hunger and thirst. Nor is there a single human being with the ability to reshape his dreams, to exchange one image for another, or to transfer his secrets from one place to another. Can what is frail and meagre in us sway the strong and mighty in us? Can the acquired self, earth-bound as it is, induce alteration and transformation in the innate Self, which is of heaven? For that Blue Flame glows immutable, transforms but is not to be transformed, dictates but cannot be dictated to.

Do you really think—you who are the most high-minded of people—that "mild sarcasm" can grow in a field sown by Pain, planted by Loneliness, and harvested by Hunger and Thirst? Do you think "philosophical jokes" can accompany a love of truth and a desire for the detached and absolute? No, my friend, you are surely above such feelings of doubt and suspicion; for doubt is the lot of the fearful and the negative, while suspicion haunts those who lack confidence in themselves. But you are strong and positive, and have abundant self-confidence. So why do you not believe in those things which fate places in the palm of your hand? And why do you not turn your gaze towards the inner beauty, which is truth, and away from the outward beauty, which is appearance?

I spent the summer months in a secluded house, set like a dream between the forest and the sea. Whenever I lost my Self in the former, I turned to the sea for rediscovery, and whenever I lost my Self in the waves, I returned to oneness with the shade of the trees. The forests of this country differ from every other forest in the world: they are green, dense, overgrown, reaching back to time immemorial, to the beginning—"In the beginning was the word, and the word was with God, and the word was God." Our sea is your sea as well, that winged voice which you hear along the coasts of Egypt is also heard by us along these coasts, and the refrain which fills *your* hearts with a life which is awesome and terrible, likewise fills *our* hearts with a life which is awesome and terrible. I have listened to the music of the sea in the East and in the West, and in both it has always been the eternal song of the infinite, taking the soul up to the heights or bringing it down to earth, at times filling it with joy, at other times with sorrow. I listened to that music on the sands of Alexandria—really, on the sands of Alexandria—in the summer of 1903, and heard then the language of the ages issuing forth from the sea of an ancient civilisation as I heard it yesterday from the sea of a modern civilisation. I first heard that language at the age of eight; I was perplexed, my life became confused, and I taxed the patience and endurance of my mother (God rest her Soul) with a barrage of questions.

I hear that same language today, and I ask all the same questions—

only now it is the "universal mother" who must answer me, and by means other than words, helping me to understand many of the things which seem to turn to silence on my lips when I try to express them to others. I sit by the sea, gazing at the furthest point of the horizon, and ask a thousand-and-one questions—the same questions I ask now that I feel like an eighty-year-old as I did when I was a boy of eight. "Is there, perhaps, anyone in your sphere who could answer?" Might not the gates of time open even for one minute so that we may perceive what mysteries and secrets lie behind them? Could you not utter one single word of "those powerful secret ordinances of life, before death draws its white veil over our faces"? You may ask whether I appreciate the benefits of a lightheartedness; I do appreciate such benefits, and my appreciation is great, but only when I translate all this into my own private language.

Strenuous effort is merely a ladder which leads us to the summit. Of course, I would rather reach my summit by flying there, but life has not taught my wings to beat and soar—so what am I to do? For I really do prefer the truth which is hidden to that which is apparent, just as I prefer that perception which is silent, complete and satisfying in itself to that which calls for analysis and justification. But I have found that an exalted silence always begins with an exalted word.

I do appreciate all the benefits [of lightheartedness], I do indeed appreciate everything in life except confusion, for if such benefits come mantled in confusion, I close my eyes and whisper to myself: "This is yet another cross for me to bear in addition to the hundred others I already bear." But being confused is not something to be abhorred in itself; it simply kept me company to a point where I grew weary of it. It became the bread I ate, the water I drank, the bed I lay on and the clothes I wore until, finding myself unable even to pronounce its name, I endeavoured to escape from its very shadow.

I think your article on *The Processions* must be the first of its kind in the Arabic language. It is the first research into what the author had in mind in writing the book.

Writers in Egypt and Syria would do well to learn from you how to discover the essence rather than the form of books, and how to explore the psychological make-up of the poet before attempting to explore the outward poetic forms. I ought not to express my personal gratitude for your psychoanalytic essay because I am aware of the objectivity with which it was written. If I were to express publicly my gratitude on behalf of our nation, it would be necessary for me to write an article about your article—something which would now seem in bad taste to our people in the East. But the day will come when I shall say what I think of May and her talents, and what I say about her will be tremendous, it will be loud and long, and it will be beautiful because it is true.

The book to be published this autumn is a volume of drawings free of "the noise of rebellion and revolt"; had it not been for the [printers'] strike it would have been out three weeks ago. Next year two books are to be published: "al-Mustawhid" ["The Lonely Man"], to which I might give another title,[1] and which contains poems and parables; the second is a book of symbolic drawings entitled "Nahwa Allah" ["Towards God"]. The latter will see me ending one phase and beginning another. As for *The Prophet*—this is a book which I thought of writing a thousand years ago, but I did not get any of its chapters down on paper until the end of last year. What can I tell you about this prophet? He is my rebirth and my first baptism, the only thought in me that will make me worthy to stand in the light of the sun. For this prophet had already "written" me before I attempted to "write" him, had created me before I created him, and had silently set me on a course to follow him for seven thousand leagues before he appeared in front of me to dictate his wishes and inclinations.

Please ask my companion and helper, the translucent element, about this prophet as he tells his story. Ask that translucent element, ask it in the silence of the night when the soul is freed from its shackles and discards its apparel, and it will reveal to you the mysteries of this prophet and the mysteries of all the prophets who preceded him.

I believe, my friend, that there is enough resolution in this translucent element for an atom of it to move a mountain; and I believe, indeed, I know, that we can extend that element like a wire between country and country, as a means by which we shall come to know all that we desire to know and achieve all that we yearn and wish for.

I have much to say about the translucent element and about the other elements as well, but I must remain silent about those others. And I shall remain silent until the mist dissolves, the gates of time open wide, and the angel of the Lord tells me: "Speak, for the time of silence is over; go forward, for your stay in the shadows of confusion has been long."

When will the gates of time open? Do you know? Do you know when the gates of time will open and the mist dissolve?

God keep you, May, and protect you always.

Sincerely,

Gibran Khalil Gibran

1 This was to become *The Forerunner*, published in 1920.

New York 15th November 1919

An envelope postmarked 15–11–19 contained the invitation card reproduced below, on which Gibran had written the following words in Arabic.

This is an invitation to an artistic banquet; would you be kind enough to honour us with your presence?

MESSRS. M. KNOEDLER & CO.

ANNOUNCE A SMALL EXHIBITION OF

FOREIGN AND AMERICAN PAINTINGS

AT THEIR GALLERIES

556-558 FIFTH AVENUE

NEAR FORTY-SIXTH ST.

NOVEMBER 27TH TO DECEMBER 16TH

Artists represented

Besnard, Bonnard, Bellows, Brush, Carriere, Cezanne, Cottet, Cadell, Calder, Daumier, Dagnan, Domingo, Gibran, Glackens, Henri, Kelly, Kronberg, La Touche, Miller, Orpen, Pissaro, Perelman, Sargent, Stevens, Sterner, Steer, Thompson, Vasquez and Weir

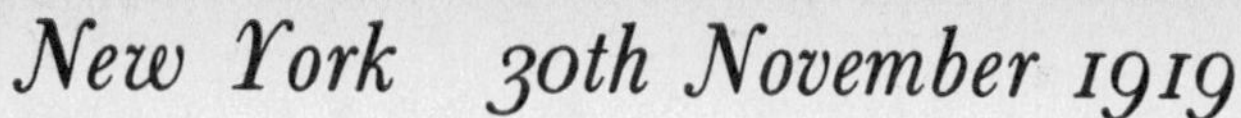

Two weeks later May received another invitation, reproduced below, this time from the Macdowell Club of New York City. Gibran had scribbled the following words in the margin, in English.

Would that you were here to lend wings to my voice and turn my mutterings into songs. Yet I shall read knowing that among the "strangers" an invisible "friend" is listening and smiling sweetly and tenderly.

THE MACDOWELL CLUB OF NEW YORK CITY

108 WEST 55TH STREET

A Club of Allied Arts

BULLETIN, NOVEMBER AND DECEMBER, 1919

The Purposes of The MacDowell Club

1. To discuss and demonstrate the principles of the arts of music, literature, the drama, painting, sculpture, and architecture, and to aid in the extension of knowledge of works especially fitted to exemplify the finer purposes of these arts, including works deserving wider recognition and to promote a sympathetic understanding of the correlation of these arts, and to contribute to the broadening of their influence, thus carrying forward the life purpose of Edward MacDowell.

2. To maintain a home for the Club in furtherance of its purposes.

Tuesday Evening, December Second

at half past eight o'clock

The Committee on Literature announces

Readings

OF

Kahlil Gibran's

Parables

AND OF

Witter Bynner's

Canticles

BY THE AUTHORS

Free to members and their guests

Would that you were here to lend wings to my voice and lure my mutterings into songs. Gibran shall read knowing that among the "strangers" an invisible "friend" is listening and smiling sweetly and tenderly.

New York 28th January 1920

My dear Miss May,

You want to know the precise meaning of my regret, and the inner secret behind my plea for forgiveness. Here then, in precise and simple terms, is what was and is behind my regret, and behind the meanings and mysteries and matters of the psyche.

I do not regret having written the letter which you refer to as my "lyric poem"—nor shall I ever have any regrets on that count.

I do not regret the smallest letter in it, nor the largest—nor shall I ever have any regrets.

I have not gone astray, and therefore see no reason why I should be redeemed. How can I regret something which continues to exist in me now exactly as it did then? For I am not one of those who regret expressing what is within themselves. Nor am I one of those who reject in their wakefulness what they can affirm in their dreams, because my dreams are my wakefulness and my wakefulness is my dreaming; and because my life is not torn between taking one step forward and two steps back.

The only sin I committed—or thought I might have committed, I who am so far removed from the world of weighing and measuring—was after reading your account of the Lebanese man who visited you before you left Cairo for the sands of Alexandria—that man on whose hands I am sorry you did not inadvertently pour some boiling water as a punishment for his indiscretion. After reading your account I noticed something I should have seen before I posted my original letter. I thought or imagined that my letter had annoyed you because I mentioned that particular incident in a letter that could be read by others. For who among us would not be annoyed and upset at the knowledge that highly personal matters had reached the hands, and been seen by the eyes, of those who have no right to such information?

This is what I belatedly noticed and now regret, and this is the only thing I ask you to deposit in the "coffer of oblivion". I referred to the system of censorship—with all the reasons for its existence and all its repercussions—as "the world of weighing and measuring". I described it thus because censorship was so very far removed from the world which occupied my thinking at that time, as far removed as hell is from heaven.

Last year I learnt something about the censor that would bring laughter to the owls among the tombs! Some of the younger employees in the Censor's Office opened all my mail from the Orient, added their own footnotes, greetings, salutations and personal observations on politics, civilisation and literature, and some even used unprecedented pretexts to request money of me.

Even stranger still, a censor in Damascus, finding some blank spaces in a letter addressed to me, embellished it with a long panegyric poem; if I were to tell you the story of this poem you would be angry with me.

But that other letter, the so-called "lyric poem", is by me, from me and in me. It is me as I was and as I shall be. The letter itself is as it was yesterday and as it will be tomorrow. So why do you not have faith and believe, [my] Doubting Thomas? Do you want to poke your finger into the wound?

Allow me to reiterate my dislike for cynicism, be it acute or oblique, between friends. I dislike joking, whether philosophical or unphilosophical, between those who have achieved a spiritual understanding. And I dislike sham and pretence in all matters, even the most exalted. The reasons for this dislike lie in the manifestations of this mechanised civilisation which I see all around me at every minute, and in the influences of this society that moves on wheels because it has no wings.

I think your imputation of "acute cynicism" in me is the outcome of something I said at one point in *The Madman*. If I am correct, then I myself must take the blame before anything else in the book because the madman is not wholly myself, the thoughts and inclinations I tried to express are by no means a complete picture of my own thoughts and inclinations; indeed the tone I chose to suit the character of the madman is not the tone I choose to adopt when sitting talking to a friend whom I love and respect. However, if you must define my reality through what I have written, what stops you from identifying me with the young man of the forest in *The Processions* instead of with the madman? My soul, May, is far more akin to the young man of the forest and to the tune of his flute than it is to the madman and his cries. And you will soon realise that the madman was nothing but a link in a long chain that was forged from a variety of metals. I do not deny that the madman was a rough link made of iron, but this does not mean that the entire chain is going to be made of coarse-grained iron. Every soul has its seasons, May; the soul's winter is not like its spring, nor is its summer like its autumn.

I was so pleased to learn that you belong to the family of Levi;[1] I was absolutely delighted, and the reason for this tremendous pleasure is that I am the son of a Maronite priest's daughter. Indeed, my maternal grandfather was a priest with a profound knowledge of theological secrets! But he was also very fond of church music and music other than that of the church, and for that reason I have forgiven his being a priest. My mother was the most beloved of his children and the one most like him. Strange that she should have resolved and prepared herself, while in the prime of her life, to enter the Nunnery of St Simon in the north of Lebanon. Ninety per cent of my character and inclinations were inherited from my mother (not that I can match her sweetness, gentleness and magnanimity), and although I do feel some antipathy towards monks, I love nuns and give them my heart's blessing. My love for them may stem from those "mystique"-filled dreams which pervaded my mother's imagination in her youth. I recall her telling me once when I was twenty:

> "It would have been better for me and for everyone else if I had entered the nunnery."
> "If you had entered the nunnery I should not have come into this world," I said.
> "You were foreordained, my son," she replied.
> "Yes, but I had chosen you for my mother long before I came into the world," I said.
> "If you had not come into the world you would have remained an angel in heaven."
> "But I am still an angel!" I replied.
> She smiled and said: "Where are your wings?"
> I held her hand and put it on my shoulder, and said: "Here".
> "They are broken!" she said.

Nine months after this conversation my mother disappeared beyond the blue horizon, but her words "they are broken" kept echoing within me, and out of these words I wove the texture of the story of *The Broken Wings*.[2]

No, May, I never belonged to my mother's earthly forebears. To me she was and still is a mother in spirit. I feel her nearness, her influence and her succour now more than I ever did before she passed away, and in a way which is quite unparalleled. This feeling, however, does not exclude the bonds that tie me to my other mothers and sisters in spirit; there is no difference between the feelings I have for my own mother and those I have for my other mothers, except the difference between clear memories and blurred memories.

I have only told you a little about my mother . . . and if we are destined ever to meet I shall tell you a great deal more about her; I am in no doubt that you will come to love her—you will love her because she loves you, as the soaring souls in that other world love the beautiful souls in this one. And you, May, are indeed a beautiful soul—so do not be surprised when I say "she loves you". The drawing published in *al-Founoon* shows her face under great emotional stress, and the one on the first page of *Twenty Drawings*[3] is her face also. I called it "Towards the Infinite" because it portrays her at the last moment of her life over here and the first moment of her life over there.

As for my father's family, I can boast three or four priests just as you boasted of priests and clergy in the Ziadah family. I will concede just one point of advantage in that your family has a greater preponderance of priests; our family tree has not produced quite such a yield. We do, however, have a priest who is a priest-and-a-half really—have you anyone of this genre? This "Khurusquf"[4] or Gibranian Monsignor prays to God, beseeching Him to bring me back into the bosom of the mother church, the all-embracing Apostolic Church, just as He brought the prodigal son back to his father! The bosom of the mother church is, as you know, similar to the bosom of our father Abraham—on the one hand for the comfort of sinners, and on the other for the repose of the dead. And the poor Christian is no sooner released from the one than he finds himself in the grip of the other; but I—thank Heaven—have never been a sinner, nor am I ever to be counted among the dead. Despite all this I do feel a certain sympathy with Abraham, and especially with Abraham's bosom. Also it should not be forgotten that half the population of North

Lebanon are priests and clergy, and the other half are the offspring of the descendants of priests! Are the people of your home-town—Ghazeer,[5] I think—anything like this? As for my home-town—Bisharri—it would be quite a task to count the number of priests and clergy there.

Yes, let us discuss *A Tear and a Smile*, for I am by no means afraid to do so! This book came out shortly before the outbreak of the war [First World War]; I sent you a copy on the day of its publication by the *al-Founoon* press, but I have had no acknowledgement of receipt from you, and this has hurt me—and I am still hurt!

As for the writings in *A Tear and a Smile*,[6] they represent early work of mine which was published in newspapers. They are the unripe grapes of my vineyard—I wrote them long before *Nymphs of the Valley*,[7] in fact they were all published in successive issues of the newspaper *al-Muhajer*[8] some sixteen years ago. It was Naseeb 'Arida who decided to collect them, adding two of my articles written in Paris twelve years ago. God forgive him! I wrote huge volumes of prose and verse in the period between childhood and adolescence! But I have never committed the crime of publishing them—nor will I ever do so. I am sending you another copy of *A Tear and a Smile* in the hope that you will look on the spirit of the work rather than the form.

I am fond of [the work of] Charles Guérin,[9] but feel nonetheless that the school to which he belonged and the tree of which he was a branch were not part of the forests sublime. French poetry in the latter half of the nineteenth century and the early twentieth century marked a twilight rather than a dawning. I believe the sculptor Rodin,[10] the painter Carrière[11] and the composer Debussy[12] all broke new ground and were truly to be numbered among the great. Until now, Guérin and his contemporaries have been following the course charted for them by the psychological conditions of the pre-war period. Despite their awareness of the beauty of life, and indeed of the pain, joy, revelations and mystery of life, they represent the twilight of an epoch rather than the dawn of a new one. I also believe that contemporary poets and writers in the Arab world represent this same idea, the same situation and the same epoch, though on a much smaller scale.

Talking of the Arab world, there is a question I should like to ask you:

Why do you not teach the poets and writers of Egypt new ways to follow? You alone have the ability to do this, so what is stopping you? You, May, are one of the daughters of the new morn—so why do you not rouse those who are sleeping? One talented maiden is, was and [always] will be equivalent to a thousand talented men. I have no doubt that were you to rally those lost and confused souls enslaved by the force of inertia, you might well stir life in them and infuse them with the resolution and aspiration to climb towards the mountain-peak. Do this, and be secure in the knowledge that he who pours oil into the lamp fills his house with light—and is not the Arab world both your house and mine?

You expressed your regret that you were unable to attend the "artistic banquet", and your regret surprises me; indeed, as a matter of fact it astonishes me. Do you not remember that we were together at the exhibition? Have you forgotten the way we moved from picture to picture? Have you forgotten how we strolled round that vast hall, searching, criticising and exploring what lay behind the lines and colours of those symbols and meanings and purposes? Have you forgotten all that? Evidently the translucent element within us acts and moves without our knowledge. It sails across the sky to the other side of the globe while we sit confined in a small room reading the evening papers; it visits distant friends while we sit talking to those of our friends who are at hand; it moves through remote, enchanted forests and fields unseen by the human eye, while we serve tea to a lady who is telling us all about her daughter's wedding.

The translucent element in us is mysterious, May, and a multitude of its activities are unknown to us. Whether we come to recognise it or not, it remains our hope and our goal; our destiny and our perfection; it is our very Selves in our divine state. I believe, therefore, that were you to exert your memory a little you would remember our visit to the exhibition—so why don't you?

My letter has grown in length—for when one finds pleasure in something, one attempts to prolong that pleasure.

I began this dialogue with you before midnight, and now I find myself in the hours between midnight and dawn, but so far I have not said one word of what I wanted to say when I began my letter. The innate reality in us, that absolute essence, that dream clothed in wakefulness expresses itself in nothing but silence.

I had every intention of asking you a thousand and one questions, but the cock has crowed and I have not asked a single question. I wanted to ask, for example, whether the word "sir" exists in the vocabulary of friendship. I searched for the word in my copy of that "dictionary" but could not find it, which left me somewhat confused; I thought my copy was the standard edition—but I may be mistaken.

This is a trivial question. I shall leave the more important questions for another occasion—for another night—because my evening has now grown "old", and I do not wish to write to you in the shadows of "old" nights.

I hope the New Year will fill the palm of your hand with stars.

May God protect you, May, and may He guard you.

Your sincere friend,

Gibran Khalil Gibran

P.S. After concluding this letter I opened my window to find the city arrayed in white, and the snow falling resolutely in abundance. It is an awe-inspiring scene, gloriously pure and untarnished, taking my thoughts back to the north of Lebanon, to the days of my childhood when I used to make shapes and figures from the snow, which melted as soon as the sun came up.

I love these showers of snow just as I love storms—I will go outside, I will walk out this very minute into the white storm. But I shall not walk alone.

Gibran

1 From Levi, the third son of Jacob, whose line provided the Judaic holy order with its priests and rabbis.

2 *The Broken Wings*, an Arabic novelette by Gibran published in 1912.

3 *Twenty Drawings*, a book of drawings by Gibran with an introduction by Alice Raphael, published in New York, 1919.

4 "Khurusquf" is a coined word from the two Arabic words *khuri* ("priest") and *usquf* ("bishop").

5 Ghazeer, a Lebanese village in Kiserwan, near the Ziadah family's home town of Shahtoul, where she used to spend the summer.

6 *A Tear and A Smile*, a collection of articles and prose poems by Gibran, published in 1914.

7 *Nymphs of the Valley*, a book published in 1906, in which Gibran attacked fanaticism.

8 *Al-Muhajer* (*The Emigrant*), an Arabic newspaper founded by Michael Rustum in the United States in 1895.

9 Charles Guérin (1873–1907), a French poet who wrote passionate, tender poems.

10 Auguste Rodin (1840–1917), the French sculptor, had a considerable influence on Gibran's style, and he is said to be the first person to have compared Gibran's work with that of William Blake. (See page 19.)

11 Eugène Carrière (1849–1906), the French painter whose paintings were famous for their misty backgrounds.

12 Claude Debussy (1862–1918), who was at the height of his fame as the leading French "Impressionist" composer.

New York 3rd November 1920

My friend May,

My recent silence has been nothing but the silence of a man who is confused and puzzled; for I have often sat in this valley between my confusion and puzzlement, wanting to speak with you and reproach you—but have found nothing to say. I found nothing to say, May, because I felt you had left nothing to be said, and because I felt you wished to sever those unseen threads spun by the invisible hand that binds thought to thought, soul to soul.

I once sat in this room and gazed at your face for a long time, without speaking a single word. You, on the other hand, stared at me, shook your head and smiled the smile of someone who revels in the confusion and puzzlement of those who happen to be in his company.

What am I to say now that I have your sweet letter in front of me? This sublime letter has turned my confusion into embarrassment. I am embarrassed about my silence, about being hurt, I am embarrassed by the pride in me that made me put my finger to my lips and remain silent. Only yesterday I considered you to be the "culprit", but today, having seen your kindness and magnanimity embrace like two angels, I consider myself the culprit.

But listen to me, dear friend, and I shall acquaint you with the reasons for my silence and my injured feelings. I possess two lives: one I spend in working, searching, meeting people and dealing with them, and probing the hidden mysteries that reside in the depths of men's hearts; the other I spend in a faraway place, quiet, awe-inspiring, full of enchantment, unconfined by either space or time. During the past year, whenever I reached that distant spot I found another soul beside my own, exchanging the minutest thoughts and sharing the deepest emotions. This I attributed at the start to fundamentals pure, and simple; but no sooner had two months passed than I began to realise the existence of a secret far beyond those fundamentals and more refined than the normal scheme of things. Equally strange was the fact that I used to return from these visits [to that spot] with a feeling that a hand with a touch like the mist had passed over my face, and sometimes I would hear a fine and gentle voice, like the breathing of a tiny infant, reverberating in my ears.

Some say I am a "visionary", but I do not know what they mean by this word. I do know, however, that I am not so much of a "visionary" that I would lie to my Self. Even if I were to do so, my Self would not believe me. This Self, May, sees nothing in life which is not of itself, and will believe nothing but what it has experienced individually. And when it experiences something, that something becomes a branch of the Self's own tree. I had an experience last year—and it was an experience, not something I dreamt; I passed through it several times, and had first-hand knowledge of it in both the mind and the senses. I experienced it and meant to keep it to myself as a secret that belonged to me; but I did not. I shared it with a [female] friend of mine. I shared it with her because I felt an urgent need to share it at that time. Do you know what my friend said to me? Immediately she said: "This is nothing but a lyric poem." If a mother carrying her child were told she had "a wooden doll" on her shoulder, and that she was carrying it with a deal of "frippery", what might her answer be? And what might she feel?

The months passed and the words "lyric poem" were indelibly inscribed on my heart. But my friend was not satisfied. And being less than satisfied she lay in wait for me, and I could not say a word without her snapping back an angry reprimand, I could see nothing of her that was not hidden by a mask, and every time I stretched out a hand she pierced it with a nail.

After that I was filled with despair. Of all the elements of the Self, nothing is more bitter than that of despair. Nothing in life is more difficult than declaring to one's Self: "You have been defeated."

Despair, May, is the lowest ebb of any heart's tide. Despair, May, is a voiceless feeling. That is why I used to sit in front of you during those long months and gaze on your face for a long time without saying a word. That is why I did not write when it was my turn to do so. That is why I used to whisper to myself: "I no longer have a role to play." But in the heart of every winter there throbs a spring, and behind the veil of each night is a smiling morn; and so my despair has been transformed into a form of hope.

What a sacred hour that was when I created my drawing "Towards the Infinite"! How awe-inspiring and sweet is the touch of a woman's lips upon the neck of another woman in meditation! How glorious is the light that emanates from our inner being, how truly glorious is that effulgent light, May!

What might I say of a man who is torn between two women: one weaving the hours of his waking out of his dreams; the other forming his dreams from the hours of his wakefulness? What might I say of a heart placed by God between two lamps? What could I say about such a man? Would I say that he is sad? I do not know; but I do know that selfishness is not a part of his sadness. Would I say that he is happy? I do not know; but I do know that selfishness is not a part of his happiness. Would I say that he is a stranger in this world? I do not know; but I ask you whether you want him to remain a stranger to you. Is he a stranger, alone and without anyone in the world who can understand a word of his language—the language of his soul? I do not know, but I ask you whether you would refuse to speak to him in that language, of which no-one has more knowledge than yourself?

Are you not also a stranger in this world? Are you not a stranger to your environment in all your aims, desires, deeds and inclinations? Tell me, tell me, May, are there many in this world who understand the language of your soul? How many times, I wonder, have you come across someone who listens to you in your silence, or who understands you in your stillness, or who accompanies you to life's Holiest of Holies while you sit in front of him in a house set in a row of other houses?

You and I are numbered among those whom God has favoured with friends, loved ones, well-wishers and a host of admirers. And yet, tell me, is there anyone among those sincere and enthusiastic friends to whom either of us could say: "Do bear my cross for one day"? Is there anyone among them who knows that behind our songs is a song that cannot be captured in sound and has no chords to which it can be set? Is there anyone among them who will ever come to know the joy of our sorrow and the sorrow of our joy?

You tell me: "You are an artist and a poet, and you should be happy being an artist and a poet." But I am neither an artist nor a poet, May. I have spent my days and my nights drawing and writing, but the "I" [that is my Self] lies neither in my days nor in my nights. I am mist, May,

I am mist that cloaks things but never unites them. I am mist unchanged into rain water. I am mist, and mist is my loneliness and my being alone, and in this is my hunger and my thirst. My misfortune, however, is that this mist is my reality, and that it longs to meet with another mist in the sky, longs to hear the words: "You are not alone, there are two of us, I know who you are."

Tell me, tell me, my friend, is there anyone in this world who would be able or willing to say to me: "I am another mist, O mist, so let us cloak the mountains and the valleys, let us wander among and over the trees, let us cover the high rocks, let us together penetrate the heart and the pores of all creation, and let us roam through those faraway places, impregnable and undiscovered"? Tell me, May, is there anyone in your sphere who would be able or willing to say one single word of this to me?

After all this, you may be expecting me to smile and "forgive".

I have done a lot of smiling this morning. I am smiling now, deep inside myself. I am smiling with all my being—and I shall continue to smile for a long time. I am smiling as if I were created to do nothing but smile. But "forgiveness" is a formidable word that devastates and wounds, forcing me to bow my head in embarrassment and awe before that noble spirit which so humbles itself, and ask her pardon. I am the sole culprit. I have been remiss in remaining silent, and in despairing—so I beg you to pardon me and forgive the wrong I have done.

It would have been more befitting to preface this discussion with a mention of *Bahithatu al-Badiya*,[1] but personal affairs do hold sway over us, and private matters possess the power to distract us from the most important or exalted of issues. I have never read an Arabic book quite like *Bahithatu al-Badiya*; I have never in my life seen two portraits drawn with such lines and [painted] with such colours. I have never in my life seen two portraits in one: the portrait of a woman writer and reformer, and the portrait of a woman who is greater than a writer and greater than a reformer. I have never in my life seen two faces so well reflected in one mirror—a woman's face half hidden by the shadow of the world, and another woman's face illumined by the rays of the sun. I say "a woman's face half hidden by the shadow of the world" because for a long time now I have felt—and still do feel—that Bahithatu al-Badiya was unable until death to break loose from her physical environment or to divest herself of all national and social influences. The other face, the Lebanese face illumined by the rays of the sun, is, I believe, that of the first Eastern woman to ascend to the ethereal temple where all spirits shake off their bodies, created as they are out of the dust of tradition and convention and the force of inertia. This is the face of the first Eastern woman to realise the Unity of Being and all that exists both seen and unseen, known and unknown. And eventually, when time has cast the writings of writers and the poetisings of poets into the abyss of oblivion, *Bahithatu al-Badiya* will remain a book to attract the interest of admiring researchers and thinkers, and of the "wakeful". You, May, are a voice crying in the wilderness; you are a divine voice, and divine voices remain reverberating in the ethereal expanse until the end of time.

Now I must answer every one of the sweet questions you have asked me. I must leave out nothing. First, the question "how am I?" I have not given much thought of late to the "how-ness of I"; I suppose, however, that I am well, despite what besets my daily life in the form of sundry distracting spirals and wheels of different shapes and sizes.

"What am I writing?" I write a line or two between nightfall and day. I say "between nightfall and day" because I spend the daylight on my large oil paintings, which I must complete before the winter's end. Had it not been for these paintings and the contract that binds me, I should have spent the winter in Paris and in the East.

"Do I work a lot?" I work the whole time, I even work when I am asleep. In my work I am as solid as a rock, but my real work is neither in painting nor in writing. Deep inside me, May, there is another dynamic intelligence which has nothing to do with words, lines or colours. The work I have been born to do has nothing to do with brush or pen.

"What colour is the suit I am wearing today?" I am in the habit of wearing two suits at the same time, one of cloth which is woven and tailored, the other made of flesh, bone and blood. But just now I am wearing a single robe, loose-fitting, long and covered with ink and paint stains, making it not unlike the robes worn by dervishes except for their cleanliness. I have divested myself in the next room of that other robe of flesh, blood and bone, something I prefer not to have about me when I speak with you.

continued

"How many cigarettes have I smoked since this morning?" How sweet this question is, and how difficult to answer. Today, May, has been a day of smoking from first to last, and I have lit more than twenty cigarettes since this morning. As far as I am concerned, smoking is a pleasure rather than an irresistible need, for a whole day could pass without my having one cigarette. Yes indeed, I have smoked over twenty cigarettes today. But you are to blame, for if I had been on my own in this "valley" I would never have smoked. But I do not want to be on my own.

As for my house, it is still without walls or roof—which of us, I ask, wants to be a prisoner? As for the seas of sand and the ethereal oceans, they are just as they were in days of yore—deep and coastless, and full of waves. The ship in which I travel those seas sails but slowly. Is there anyone who is able or willing to give my ship an extra sail? Who is able or willing, I wonder?

As for the book "Towards God", this is still somewhat hazy in form, and the best drawings in it are still sketches in mid-air and images drawn on the face of the moon. *Al-Mustawhid*, on the other hand, came out three weeks ago under the title *The Forerunner*,[2] a copy of which I have sent you. Under the same cover I mailed you a copy of *al-'Awasif (The Tempests)*[3] and a third copy of those unripe grapes from my vineyard, *A Tear and a Smile*. I did not send you my publisher's summer list because I was away in the country during the summer—there is another reason as well! And as for the drawings, the pottery, the glass, the old books, the musical instruments and the Egyptian, Greek and Gothic statues—all of these are just as you know them to be, manifestations of that eternal and undying spirit, words taken from God's book. I have often sat before all these and pondered on the longing created within me by them; often gazed at them until they disappeared before my very eyes to be replaced by the ancient ghosts which brought them from the invisible world into the visible. I have not yet obtained the Chaldean black-stone statue. Last spring an English friend with the British Expedition in Iraq wrote and told me: "If I find anything it is yours."

I have answered all your questions, and have not left out a single one. I have reached this stage in my letter without having said one word of what I wanted to say when I started the first page. The mist in me has not turned to rain-water, and the silence, that winged and trembling silence, has not turned into speech. Will you not fill your hands with this mist? Will you not close your eyes and listen to these utterances of silence? Will you not pass by this valley again, where loneliness hovers like a bird, moves like sheep, flows like a stream and stands tall like an oak-tree? Will you not pass this way once more, May? God protect and guard you.

Gibran

1 *Bahithatu al-Badiya* (*The Desert Researcher*), a pen-name of the female Egyptian writer Malak H. Nassif (1886–1918), used as the title of a book about her by May, published in 1920 by *Dar al-Hilal*.

2 *The Forerunner*, Gibran's second English book, published in 1920, shows the same traits as his first, *The Madman*, and illustrates his deep sufi tendency.

3 *Al-'Awasif (The Tempests)*, a collection of articles, short stories and prose poems written in Arabic newspapers and magazines, published between 1912 and 1918.

Boston 11th January 1921

May,

We have reached a mountain-top, and below us are spread plains, forests and valleys, so let us sit awhile and talk a little. We cannot stay here very long because in the distance I see a higher peak, which we must reach before sunset; but we shall not leave this place until you are happy, nor take a single step forward until you have peace of mind.

We have surmounted a formidable obstacle, not without a certain amount of confusion, and I confess that I have been persistent and overpressing, but my persistence was the foreseeable result of something stronger than so-called will. I also confess that I have acted without wisdom in certain matters—are there not spheres of life which are beyond the reach of wisdom? Do we not have in us something before which wisdom turns to stone? Were my present experiences in any way like those of the past I would not have described them—but they are all strange and new, and have come all of a sudden. And had I been in Cairo and said this to you simply by word of mouth, in that detached manner without a trace of selfish ends, no misunderstanding would have arisen between us. But I was not in Cairo at that time, and there was no means of communication with you other than by letter—and writing letters on subjects such as these tends to complicate the simplest of issues and throw a heavy veil of formality over the most elemental of matters. For how often, when we want to express a simple thought, do we put it in whatever words come to us, words such as our pens are accustomed to pouring out on paper, and the result is usually a "prose poem" or a "reflective essay". The reason for this is that we feel and think in a language that is more honest and more sincere than the language in which we write. Of course we like poems, be they in prose or in verse, and we like essays both reflective and non-reflective. But free, undying passion is one thing; letter-writing is something quite else. Ever since my schooldays I have tried as far as possible to avoid using platitudes because I felt—and still feel—that they obscure both thoughts and feelings much more than they ever express them. But it appears to me now that I have not altogether escaped the very thing I abhor—it seems to me that the year and a half which has passed finds me still where I was at the age of fifteen, proof of which lies in this misunderstanding which may have resulted from my letters.

I repeat that had I been in Cairo we should have reflected awhile upon the meaning of our personal experiences as we might upon the sea or the stars or a blossoming apple-tree. For no matter how strange and unique our experiences, they are no wise more strange or unique than the sea, the stars and the blossoming apple-tree. Strange that we should accept the miracles of the earth and of space, but at the same time tend not to believe the miracles that are wrought in our souls.

I used to think, May, indeed I still think that some of our experiences cannot occur unless two people share in them jointly and simultaneously. This mode of thinking may have been the main reason why some of my letters have induced you into thinking that "we must stop here". Thank God we did not "stop there". For life, May, does not stop in one place, and the mighty procession with all its beauty cannot but march forward from one sempiternity to another. As for you and me, for us who sanctify life and tend toward what is right, blessed, sweet and noble in life with all our being, who hunger and thirst after the permanent and everlasting in life—we do not wish to say or do anything that breeds fear or "fills the soul with thorns and bitterness". We are neither able nor willing to touch the sides of the altar save with hands that have been purified by fire. And when we love a thing, May, we look on love as a goal in itself and not as a means to achieve some other end; and if we show reverence and submission before the sublime, it is because we regard submission as elevation and reverence as a form of recompense. If we long for something, we consider longing a gift and a bounty in itself. We also know that the remotest matters are those most befitting and most worthy of our longing and our inclinations. In truth we two—you and I—cannot stand in the light of the sun and say: "We must spare ourselves torment we can well do without." We cannot do without that which infuses the soul with a sacred leaven, nor can we do without the caravan which takes us to God's city; indeed we cannot do without that which brings us nearer to our Greater Selves and reveals to us the power, mystery and wonder we have within our souls. Moreover we are capable of finding intellectual happiness in the simplest manifestations of the soul; for in a simple flower we find all the glory and beauty of spring, in the eyes of the infant suckling we find all the hope and aspiration of mankind. Yet we are unwilling to use those things nearest to us as a means to reach what lies far ahead. We are neither able nor inclined to stand in front of life and state our conditions [by saying]: "Give us what we want or give us nothing—what we want or nothing at all." No, May, we do not do this, because we realise that what is right and blessed and permanent in life does not follow our wishes, but moves *us* according to its will. What motive could we have for revealing one of the secrets of our souls across the seven thousand miles that separate us, save the joy of revealing that secret? What other motive could we have for standing before the gates of the temple, except the glory of standing there? What motive does a bird have when it bursts into song, or incense when it burns? For a lonely soul may only have limited aspirations.

How sweet are your birthday wishes to me, and how delicate their fragrance. But let me tell you a little story, May, and you may laugh awhile at my expense. Naseeb 'Arida, wishing to collect the articles of *A Tear and a Smile* [and publish them] in one volume—this was before the war—decided to append that assortment of meagre pieces with the article "My Birthday", to which title he would add the [appropriate] date. As I was not in New York at the time, he began searching for my date of birth—he is an indefatigable researcher—until he eventually identified that date in the distant past, and translated the English "6th January" into "Kanoon al-Awal 6th"![1] In this way he reduced the span of my lifetime by [nearly] a year, and delayed the real day of my birth by a month! To this day, ever since the publication of *A Tear and a Smile*, I have enjoyed two birthday celebrations each year; the first was the result of an error in translation, though what error in the ethereal world really caused it I do not know! As for the year of which I have been robbed—God knows, and you know, that I paid a heavy price for it. I paid for it with the throbs of my heart, I paid for it with seventy [ton] weights of silent pain and longing for a thing unknown—so how could I allow a mere error in a book to rob me of that one year?

I am far away from the "valley", May. I arrived in this city—Boston—ten days ago to do some painting, and had they not sent me a parcel containing mail sent to my New York address, I should have lived through ten more days without your letter. This letter has untied a thousand knots in the rope of my life, and turned the desert of "waiting" into gardens and orchards—for "waiting" is the indelible etchings of time, May, and I am continually in a state of "waiting". Sometimes it seems to me that I spend my life in expectation of that which has not yet come to pass—how like the blind and the disabled who were lying by the pool at Bethesda in Jerusalem: "For an angel went down at a certain season into the pool, and troubled the water: whosoever then first after the troubling of the water stepped in was made whole of whatsoever disease he had."[2] However, now that my own angel has troubled the waters in the pool and I have found someone to put me into those waters, I walk in that enchanted and awe-inspiring spot, my eyes filled with light and my feet strengthened with firm resolve. I walk side by side with a shadow more beautiful and more lucid than the reality of all men. I walk [with my hand] holding a hand that is silken and yet strong, with a will of its own; a hand whose fingers are soft and yet capable of lifting weights and breaking heavy chains. And every now and then I turn my head to behold a pair of glittering eyes and lips touched by a smile that wounds with its sweetness.

I once told you that my life is divided into two lives, and that I spend the one in working and being with people, the other in the mist. But that was yesterday, for now my life has been unified, and I work in the mist, meet people in the mist, even sleep, dream and wake up in the mist. It is indeed an ecstasy surrounded by the beating of wings, for in that state of ecstasy loneliness is *not* loneliness, and the pain of longing for the unknown is more pleasant than anything I have known. It is a divine trance, May—a divine trance which brings near that which is remote, uncovers that which is hidden, and illuminates all things. I realise that life without this spiritual trance is but the chaff without the wheat, and I aver that all we say, do or think is worthless when compared to a single minute spent in the mist.

You want the words "lyric poem" etched on my heart! You want to use this against me so that you may take revenge against this frail form of which I am the carrier and the carried. Let it etch and etch and etch, then, and let us invoke all the lyric poems that are embedded in the ether, and let us command them to spread out over this "land" and dig canals, build roads, erect palaces, towers and temples, turn the wilderness into gardens and vineyards because a mighty people are come to inhabit it, and have chosen it as their home. You, May, are a great and mighty nation of conquerors, and at the same time you are a little girl of seven, laughing in the sun's rays, chasing butterflies, gathering rose-buds and leaping over streams. Nothing in life is sweeter to me than running after that sweet little girl, catching her and giving her a piggy-back home so that I can tell her tales that are strange and full of wonder—until slumber touches her eyelids and she falls asleep in quiet and heavenly fashion.

Gibran

1 *Kanoon-al-Awal* (literally "the 1st Kanoon") is the month of December, and January is *Kanoon al-Thani* (literally "the 2nd Kanoon").

2 The reference is to the Gospel of St. John V: 4.

New York 6th April 1921

. . . Is it well advised for a woman in her excellence to veil and hide her heart and herself from the eyes and the sight of people? God has sent you to us as a mind and a spirit. We are in dire need of the light of your face and the fire of your mind, so why do you not give us both simultaneously?

And now we have finished that bloody battle, father, brother, companion and your friend—together with the other members of the family—all ask you to turn your heart and soul into prose and poetry in the form of verses and *muwashah*,[2] and to stand as the priestess stands before the altar, even if only once every two months, and speak of that enchanting world which lies behind the worlds of thought, of science, of research and of logic.

A piece of fresh news: I have obtained a first-rate telescope, and I spend an hour or two every evening staring into infinity, close to that which is distant and remote, and in awe of the Greater Whole. It is midnight now, and Orion has reached its point in the celestial sphere. And you know, Mary,[3] that the nebula near the orbit of Orion is the most beautiful and awe-inspiring spectacle in outer space. So let us rise now, my companion, and go up onto the roof to gaze at the night-sky and the beauty of wonderment, of compassion and of knowledge in the eyes of the angels. I say, dear lady, that a man's life will stay like a desert—empty except for sand—until God endows him with a daughter such as my little princess. And I also say, dear lady, that he who does not have a daughter should adopt one, because the secret and meaning of time are hidden in the hearts of young girls.

I call my daughter "princess" because every movement and gesture she makes, the harmony in her voice, her smile, her pranks, her ingenuity—all these indicate a royal character. Moreover she is despotic and holds firmly to her own ideas, without anyone being able to change or modify them—but sweet indeed is her despotism and her absolute judgment.

This is a short letter—a very short letter—but it is the first I have written for five weeks. Will you have read into it what was not written

down? I shall write again when I wake up [in the morning]. Spring will take me by the hand and pull me out from under my bedclothes and lead me to green pastures where life gives her children new heart, and changes their whisperings and breathings into songs and hymns of praise.

Please, May my friend, do not be displeased with me—I beg you not to be displeased with me. Bless me a little, for I bless you always.

Gibran

1 The first two pages of this letter are missing.

2 A form of Arabic poetry which was developed in Arab Spain (al-Andalus).

3 Mary was May's original name, but she chose the latter because it was more poetic.

New York
Evening of Saturday, 21st May 1921

May, my friend,

"With much affection—and again with much affection"—this is a simple statement of truth which has only recently become clear to me, opening new doors and windows in front of my spirit. Once I realised what had happened I found myself confronted by sights that I had never dreamed existed in this world.

"With much affection—and again with much affection"—and from the "much" and the "affection" I have learnt to pray in joy and yearn in peace, and to be resigned without humiliation. I have come to realise that the lonely man is capable of filling his loneliness with the light of that word "much" and of dispelling fatigue with the sweetness of "affection". I have come to realise that the lonely man who is a stranger is able to become a father, a brother, a companion and a friend—and, above all, to be a child enjoying life as well. "With much affection"—in this "much" and in this "affection" are wings that spread and hands that bless.

My health is better than it was a month ago, but I am still unwell. And this frail body is still lacking in order, balance and rhythm. You want me to tell you what is wrong with me, so here is what the doctors say:

> Nervous prostration caused by overwork and lack of nourishment. General disorder of the system. Palpitation was an inevitable result. Pulse beats 115 per minute—the normal is about 80.

In the past two years, May, I have overburdened my body. I used to paint for as long as there was daylight, then write until morning, give lectures and meet all kinds of people—this last activity being the most difficult thing under the sun. At the dining-table I used to busy myself conversing with those who liked talking until the time came for coffee to be served, when I would gulp a great deal of this down and be satisfied with it in place of food and drink. How often I used to return home after midnight and, instead of complying with what God has ordained as normal behaviour for our bodies, would rouse myself with cold showers and strong coffee, and spend the rest of the night [absorbed in] writing or painting—as though I was crucified. If only I had been like my fellow North Lebanese the illness would not have had me in its grip so quickly. They are robust and strong in physique, whereas I am the opposite, having failed to inherit any of the physical virtues of those sturdy folk. I have taken up a lot of time and space in talking about my illness. I should have preferred not to, but what else can I do when I have no alternative but to answer every one of your questions, questions so full of sweet concern, "benevolence and solicitude"?

Where is this long letter, written in pencil on square-ruled paper in the form of a crossword, and composed in a beautiful garden looking out over a long line of river-boats?* Where is my letter, May? Why have you not sent it to me? I am eager to receive it, and I want all of it, every little bit of it. Do you know how much I desire to receive that letter after having read a brief snatch of it—a divine fragment which arrived to announce the dawning of a new day? Do you know that, had it not been for my apprehension about using the words "with madness", I would have cabled you last night imploring you to post the letter?

Do you discern any goodness in me, May? And are you in need of goodness? Your words wound with their sweetness, so what should my answer be? If in my being there should be anything you need, my friend, then it is yours in its entirety. Goodness is not a virtue in itself; its opposite is ignorance. Can ignorance reside where there is "much affection"?

If goodness consists in loving what is beautiful, in feeling awe in the presence of what is noble, and in longing for the distant and unseen—if goodness be all these things, then I am one of those people who possess goodness. But if it lie in things other than these, then I do not know who or what I am. I feel, May, that the perfect woman must demand the existence of goodness in the soul of a man, even if he is ignorant.

How much I should like to be in Egypt now. How much I should like to be in my own country, near those I love. Do you know, May, every day I imagine myself in a house in the suburbs of an Oriental city, and I imagine my friend sitting in front of me reading aloud the latest of her as yet unpublished articles, and we spend a long time discussing its subject before agreeing that this is the best thing she has written so far. I also imagine that, following this, I would take out some papers from underneath the pillows on my bed and read out a passage I had written the night before, and this would meet with the mild approval of my friend, although to herself she would say: "He should never write when he is in this condition. The structure of the piece reveals weakness, frailty and confusion—he should not indulge in any intellectual exertion until he is fully cured." My friend would say this to herself and I should hear the words in myself, becoming partly convinced of the truth of what she says; after which I would say in a loud voice: "Give me a chance, allow me a week or two and I will read you a most beautiful piece." To this you would then retort: "You should refrain from writing, painting or any other activity for a year or two, and if you do not so refrain I shall be most displeased with you." My friend utters the word "displeased" in a tone of "absolute despotism" and then she gives me an angelic smile, so that I am for a while perplexed by her displeasure and her smile; and then I find myself delighted with her displeasure and her smile—and delighted even with my own perplexity.

Talking of writing, do you know the measure of joy, pride and happiness I have derived from those articles and short stories of yours which have appeared in the past months? I have not read a single piece by you without my heart swelling [with joy]; and on reading them for a second time I find all the generalities seem to change into something of personal significance, and I trace in the ideas and structure what no other person could see or read between the lines—lines which have been written for no-one but me. You are, May, a treasure among the treasures in life—nay, you are more than that—you are you. And I thank God that you are of that nation to which I, too, belong, and that you live at a time in which I live also. Whenever I imagine you living in the last century or the next, I raise my hand and sweep the air like someone brushing a cloud of smoke away from his face.

In two or three weeks' time I am to go to the country to live in a small house, built of dreams between the sea and the forest. How beautiful that forest is, and how abundant her flowers and birds and springs! Some years ago I used to wander all alone in that forest; and I used to go down to the sea-shore and sit sadly on the rocks, or else plunge into the waves like a man wishing to escape the world and its ghosts. But this summer I shall stroll through the forest and sit by the sea and find in my soul something to help me forget loneliness, and in my heart something to distract me from sadness.

Tell me, May, what will you do this summer? Are you going to Ramleh in Alexandria, or to Lebanon? Are you going alone to our Lebanon? Oh, when will *I* return to Lebanon? Can you tell me when I may ever be freed from this country and from the golden chains which my desires have shackled around my neck?

Do you remember, May, once telling me that a journalist in Buenos Aires had written to ask for your picture and for one of your articles? I have thought many times of the request of that journalist, the request of all newspapermen. Each time I have said with regret: "I am not a journalist! I am not a journalist! It is therefore not possible for me to make the same requests as journalists. If I were the owner of a magazine, or an editor, I should be free to ask for her picture without embarrassment or fear, and without a preamble embroidered in trembling words." All this I said, and still say in my heart. May those who have taken my heart as their home heed my words.

It is midnight, and until now I have not put down on paper the word my lips pronounce, sometimes in a whisper and at other times in a loud voice. I place the word I wish to utter in the very heart of silence; for silence preserves all that we say with affection, with zeal, and with faith. And silence, May, carries our prayers to wherever we wish, or else raises them to God.

I am going to bed now, and I shall have a long sleep tonight. I shall tell you in my dreams what I have not spelt out on paper. Good night, May. May God protect you.

Gibran

* I can see the river-boats in my mind's eye because I remember them from my visit to Egypt [Gibran's own footnote].

New York
The Morning of Monday, 30th May 1921

May, Mary, my friend,

I have just woken up after a strange dream. In that dream I heard you speak words to me, but in a stern and scathing tone. What bothered me in the dream, however—and is still bothering me greatly—is that I saw a small wound in your forehead, and it was dripping with blood. Nothing in our lives is more worthy of thought and contemplation than the dreams we have, and I am a man who dreams a lot. But I forget my dreams unless they are about those whom I love. I do not remember ever having dreamed a clearer dream than this, which is why I am confused, perturbed and worried this morning. What does the stern and scathing tone of your words signify? What is the meaning of the wound in your forehead? And is there anybody who can tell me what lies behind my gloom and sadness?

I shall spend my day saying prayers in my heart. I shall pray for you in the silence of my heart, and I shall pray for both of us.

May God bless and protect you.

Gibran

New York 9th May 1922

My esteemed friend,[1]

You inquire of me, madam, whether I be lonely in thought, heart or spirit. How then am I to answer you? I feel my loneliness to be no greater nor more profound than the loneliness of others. Everyone is lonely and on his own. Each one of us is an enigma. Each one of us is veiled with a thousand veils, and what difference is there between one lonely person and another, except that one speaks of his loneliness while another keeps it to himself? In talk there may be some comfort, while in silence there may be some virtue.

I do not know, madam, whether my loneliness with all its sadness is but a manifestation of the "whims of my *persona*", or a proof that there is no personality in the being I call "I". No, I do not know. However, if loneliness be a sign of weakness, then I am certainly the weakest of men.

With regard to my article entitled "My Self is Laden with its Own Fruits";[2] it was not "the sigh of the poet in a moment of passing grief"; it was "an echo of a common, old, established feeling which many have experienced and are experiencing". And you, my lady, know this is sometimes a quality that is not free from pride or conceit, but which is nonetheless natural.

You put it well: "In the middle of a crowd the pain and suffering of loneliness are merely intensified." This is an essential truth. For how often does a man find himself among his fellows and well-wishers, talking to them, exchanging ideas, sharing in their thoughts and actions, and all this he does sincerely and wholeheartedly, yet failing to transcend the limitations of the acquired self in a world of appearance; as for his other Self, the hidden Self, it stays silent and alone in the world of its origin.

Most people, and here I include myself, are fond of smoke and ashes; but they fear fire because it dazzles the eyes and burns the fingers. Most people, and again I include myself, are engrossed in dealing with one another only on a superficial level; they ignore the essence because it never comes within their faculties of perception. It is not easy for a man to tear his heart out in order for others to see what is hidden there. And this, madam, is loneliness, and this is sadness.

I purposely expressed myself incorrectly when I told you towards the end of last summer: "For six weeks I have been trying to write to you." I should have said: "For six weeks I have been hiring people to take care of my letters because the nerves of my right hand were unfit for any writing." But it never occurred to me that the word "trying" would become a scalpel in the hands of my friend. I used to be under the illusion that the winged soul could never be imprisoned in a cage of words, and that the mist could never turn to stone. I used to dream and dream, and found comfort in my reveries. But when the dawn broke and I woke up, I would find myself sitting on top of a heap of ashes with a bruised reed in my hand and a crown of thorns on my head . . . No matter, I am to blame. It is I who must take the blame, May.

I hope your desire to visit Europe will be fulfilled. You will find much to please and delight you there in the field of art and technology, especially in Italy and France. There are museums and academies, there are ancient Gothic cathedrals, there are the relics of two centuries of the Renaissance, the fourteenth and fifteenth centuries, and there is the best of what has been left us by those conquered and forgotten nations of the world. Europe, madam, is a den of thieves—experts and connoisseurs who are fully aware of the value of precious things and the way to go about purchasing them.

I had intended to return to the East next autumn, but after some thought I realised that being a stranger among strange people is much easier to bear than being a stranger among my own kindred. I am not a man who is inclined to take the easy way out; and there are patterns to follow even in madness and despair.

Please accept my greetings accompanied by my sincerest best wishes, and may God protect you.

Yours sincerely,

Gibran Khalil Gibran

1 An Arabic form of address. The whole letter is deliberately over-formal and ironic.

2 The article appeared in Arabic under the title "Nafsi Muhamalatun bi Athmar-iha", later included in *al-Badayi'wa'l-Tarayif* (*Rare and Beautiful Sayings*) published in 1923.

No, May, the tension does not exist in those meetings when the mist envelops us, but in the meetings when we converse. When I meet you in that distant and quiet field I always find you a sweet and kind maid who is conscious of all things and knows all things, who gazes upon life through God's light and who fills life with the light of her own spirit. But whenever we meet in the blackness of ink and the whiteness of paper I find you and myself to be the most quarrelsome of adversaries engaged in a duel—a duel of the intellect consisting of nothing but finite measurements and limited results.

May God forgive you, you have robbed me of my heart's tranquillity, and had it not been for my steadfastness and obduracy you would have robbed me of my faith. It is strange that those nearest to us are [also] those most capable of confusing and disturbing our lives for us.

We must not reprove one another, we must come to an understanding, and we cannot reach an understanding unless we speak with childlike candour. We are both inclined to make use of rhetoric with all its demands of skill, ingenuity, embellishment and organisation. You and I have come to realise that friendship and rhetoric are not easily combined. The heart is simple, May, and the manifestations of the heart are rudimentary things, whereas rhetoric is a social vehicle. So will you agree that we should switch from rhetoric to simple talk?

"You live in me and I in you, you know this and I know it too."

Are not these few words far better than everything we have said in the past? What prevented us from uttering such words last year? Was it embarrassment, pride, social conventions, or what? From the start we have known this fundamental truth, so why have we not shown it with the openness that characterises devout and dedicated believers? Had we done so, we could have spared ourselves doubt, pain, regret, indignation and vexations—vexations which turn the honey of the heart into bitterness, and the bread of the heart into dust. May God forgive both you and me.

We must come to an understanding. But how can we achieve this

continued

unless each of us believes wholly in the other's frankness? I tell you, Mary, I tell you before heaven and earth and what lies between them, I am not one of those who write "lyric poems" only to send them as private epistles from the West to the East. Nor am I one of those who in the morning speak as if they were laden with fruit, and in the evening forget themselves, the fruit and the weight of the fruit. I am not one of those who touch what is holy without first cleansing their fingers with fire. Nor am I one of those who, sensing the vacuum of their days and nights, fill them with philanderings. I am not one of those who belittle the secrets of their souls and what is hidden in their hearts only to publicise them to any wind that blows. It is true that I am a very industrious man; and I yearn for whatever is great, noble, beautiful and pure in just the same way as those others who yearn after greatness, nobility, beauty and purity. But I am also a stranger among men, entirely on my own, just like those other men who are entirely on their own despite possessing seventy thousand friends of both sexes. Also I am not inclined, just as certain other men are inclined, to indulge in the sexual athletics known to many by mellifluous adjectives and given seductive-sounding names. For, like our fellow neighbour, May, I am a lover of God, of life, and of humanity; and even to this day fate has not demanded any action from me that it would shame our fellow neighbour to perform.

When I first wrote to you my letter was a proof of the confidence I have in you, but when you sent your reply it was a proof of your doubt. I felt compelled to write to you, but you replied with caution. I spoke to you of a strange truth, and in answer you said affably: "Well done, clever boy, how wonderful your lyric poems are!" I know all too well that I did not observe familiar etiquette, but I have never observed nor will I ever observe familiar etiquette. I also know that your caution was for fear of what might develop, and that the cause of my agony is that I did not anticipate what might come. Had I written to anyone other than May I should have foreseen what would happen; but could I have revealed the truth to anyone but May? It is strange that I felt no regret after it. I felt no regret, but remained firm in the truth within me and eager to reveal it to you. So I wrote to you frequently and each time I received a cordial reply, but the reply came from someone other than the May I knew. I used to receive those cordial replies from May's secretary, who is an intelligent young woman living in Cairo, Egypt. I cried out and whispered words of reverence; I received a reply; yes, I received a reply, but not from the one "in whom I live and who lives in me", but from a woman who is cautious and pessimistic, and who gives and takes as if I were the accused and she the accuser.

Am I angry with you? Not at all, I am only angry with your secretary. Have I then passed verdict justly or unjustly on you?

Not at all, I have never judged you. My heart will not and cannot allow you to stand trial. My heart will not and cannot allow me to sit in judgment on you. What we share, May, removes us from all courtrooms. But as regards your secretary I do have an opinion: whenever you and I sit down to talk, she comes in and seats herself in front of us, exactly as if she were preparing to record the minutes of a political conference. I ask you, I ask you, my friend, do we really need your secretary? Because if so I shall call in my secretary since I too wish to be efficient. Do you want my secretary to be in attendance?

Look, May: here are two mountain children ascending towards the rays of the sun, and over there are four people, a woman and her secretary, and a man and his secretary. Here are two children walking hand in hand according to God's will and towards a destination willed by God; and over there are four people sitting in an office quibbling and arguing among themselves, standing up and sitting down, each trying to prove what he or she believes to be right by condemning what he or she believes to be wrong with the other person. Here are two children, over there four people, so which way is your heart inclined? Tell me which way?

Oh, I wish you knew how weary I am of this unnecessary confusion; if you only knew how much I need simplicity. I wish you knew how much I long for the absolute, the white absolute, the absolute in the storm, the absolute on the cross, the absolute that cries but does not hide its tears, and the absolute that laughs and is not embarrassed by its laughter—I wish you knew, I wish you knew.

"What would I like to do this evening?"

The time is not evening: it is two o'clock in the morning, where do you want us to go at this late hour? Better that we should stay here, here in this stillness. Here we can express our longing, until that longing brings us nearer to the heart of God. Here we can love humanity until humanity opens its heart to us.

Sleep has kissed your eyes. Do not deny that sleep has kissed your eyes. I have seen him kissing them, I have seen him kiss them like this, this way! So put your head here, on this shoulder and sleep; sleep, my little one, sleep, for you are at home in your homeland.

I, on the other hand, will remain awake; I shall stay awake by myself, I must keep vigil until the morning. I was born to keep vigil until the morning. May God guard you, may God bless my vigil, may God protect you always.

Gibran

Boston 3rd November 1923

An envelope postmarked 3–11–23 contained a postcard of a Michelangelo sculpture, with the following message.

Look, Mary, how great Michelangelo is. This man, who has created a host of mighty giants out of marble, can be sweet and gentle in the extreme. What a good illustration Michelangelo's life is of the fact that real strength is the daughter of gentleness, and that flexibility is the offspring of true resolve.

Good night to the pretty face.[1]

Gibran

1 The phrase is a peculiarly Arabic form of endearment which has no exact English equivalent.

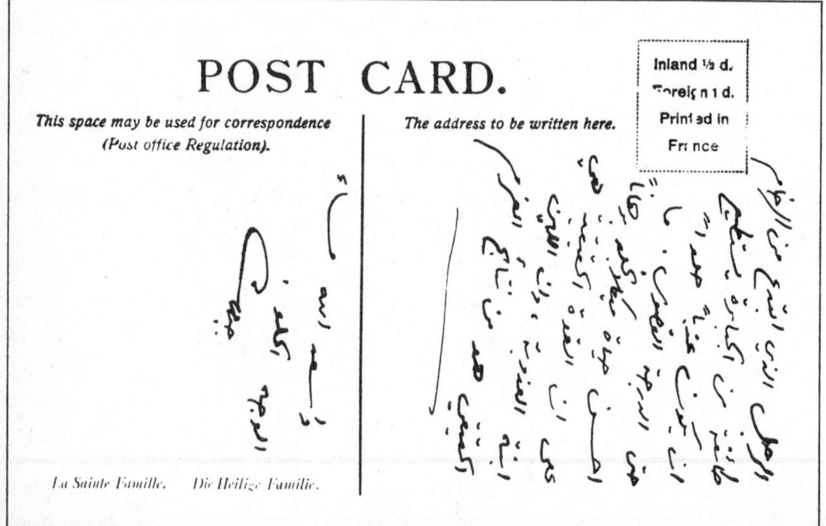

BUONAROTI — The Madonna, Infant Christ, St. John the Baptist,
THE NATIONAL GALLERY, LONDON

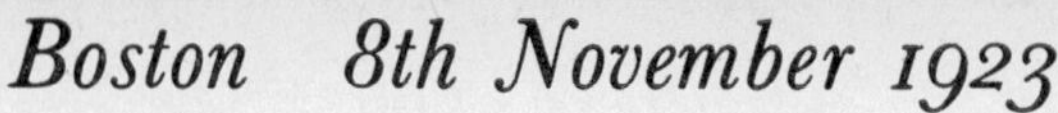

Boston 8th November 1923

An envelope postmarked 8–11–23 contained two postcards with the following message.

Tell me whether you have ever in your life seen anything more beautiful than these two faces. I believe they are the most sublime expression of Greek art at its zenith. Whenever I visit the city of Boston I pay a visit to its museum, making my way directly to the "Grecian Room", and sit for an hour studying the two faces. I then leave the museum without a glance either to the left or right, in order not to offend that divine beauty by looking at any other beauty.

And good morning to the sweet and pretty face.

Gibran

continued

POST CARD.

PLACE STAMP HERE.
DOMESTIC ONE CENT
FOREIGN TWO CENTS

THIS SPACE FOR MESSAGE. FOR ADDRESS ONLY.

(١)

قولي لي ... هذين الوجهين في
حياتك؟ في عقيدتي انها ارتسم ...
... عندما كان الفن اليوناني على قمة
اكبر. كلما زرت ... مدينة بوسطن اذهب

HEAD FROM CHIOS
GREEK. FOURTH CENTURY. B. C.
MUSEUM OF FINE ARTS, BOSTON, MASS.
COPR. DETROIT PUBLISHING CO.

"PHOSTINT" CARD. MADE ONLY BY DETROIT PUBLISHING CO.
TRADE MARK - REG. U.S. PAT. OFF.
60301

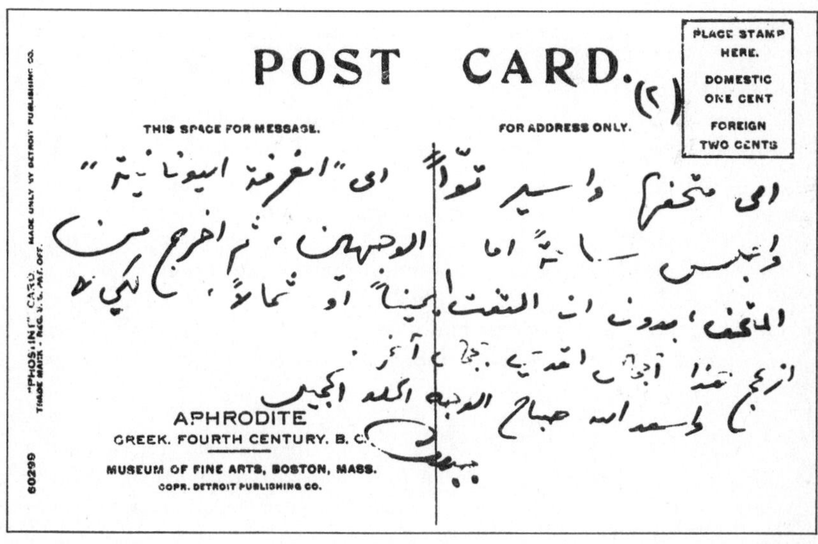
POST CARD.

PLACE STAMP HERE.
DOMESTIC ONE CENT
FOREIGN TWO CENTS

THIS SPACE FOR MESSAGE. FOR ADDRESS ONLY.

(٢)

الى متحف ... الى "الغرفة اليونانية"
واجلس ... امام الوجهين، ثم اخرج من
المتحف، بدون ان التفت يمينا او شمالا، لكي
ارجع غدا ...
... الله صباح ... الكلمة ...
جبران

APHRODITE
GREEK. FOURTH CENTURY. B. C.
MUSEUM OF FINE ARTS, BOSTON, MASS.
COPR. DETROIT PUBLISHING CO.

"PHOSTINT" CARD. MADE ONLY BY DETROIT PUBLISHING CO.
TRADE MARK - REG. U.S. PAT. OFF.
60299

New York 1st–3rd December 1923

How sweet your letter is to my heart, May, how sweet it is to my heart.

I went to the countryside five days ago, and I have spent those five days saying farewell to the autumn I love, returning to this "valley" only two hours ago. I returned frozen and perished because I made the journey in a convertible car, covering a distance greater than that between Nazareth and Bisharri . . . But . . . I returned to find your letter on top of a pile of other letters, and you know that all other mail vanishes before my eyes when I receive a letter from my little beloved. I sat down and read it and derived warmth from it. I then changed my clothes and read it a second time, and then again a third time, and I continued to read it to the exclusion of everything else. I do not mix divine wine with any other juice, Mary.

At this hour you are with me; you are with me, May. You are here, here, and I am talking to you, but with words better than these by far. I speak to your great heart in a language greater than this, and I know that you hear me, I know that we understand one another clearly and lucidly, and I know that we are nearer God's throne on this night than at any time in the past.

I praise and thank God, I praise and thank God; for the estranged [one] has returned to his homeland and the traveller to the home of his father and mother.

At this very moment a glorious thought, a most glorious thought strikes me. Listen, my sweet little one: if we should ever quarrel hereafter (that is, if quarrelling be unavoidable) we must not go our separate ways as we used to in the past after every "battle". We must remain, despite our differences, under one roof until we are bored with quarrelling and begin to laugh; or else until quarrelling itself is bored with us and leaves us with a shake of the head.

What do you think of this idea?

So let us quarrel as much as we like, or as much as quarrelling itself will allow us, for you are from Ihdin and I from Bisharri, and quarrelling between us is therefore traditional. However, no matter what happens in the days ahead we must look into each other's faces until the clouds pass over. And if your secretary or my secretary should come in—for they are the cause of our quarrels—we must gently usher them out, but with the utmost dispatch.

Of all people you are the nearest to my soul, and the nearest to my heart, and our souls and hearts have never quarrelled. Only our thoughts have quarrelled, and thought is acquired, it is derived from the environment, from what we see in front of us, from what each day brings to us; but soul and heart formed a sublime essence in us long before our thoughts. The function of thought is to organise and arrange, and this is a good function and necessary for our social lives, but it has no place in the life of the heart and soul. "If we should quarrel hereafter we must not go our separate ways." Thought can say this despite being the cause of all quarrelling, but it cannot utter one word about love, nor is it able to measure the soul in terms of words, nor to weigh the heart in the scales of its logic.

I love my little one, but I do not know in my mind why I love her. I do not want to know in my mind, it is sufficient that I love her. It is sufficient that I love her in my soul and in my heart. It is sufficient for me to rest my head on her shoulder when I am sad, lonely and in solitude, or when I am happy, entranced and full of wonder. It is sufficient for me to walk by her side to the top of the mountain and to tell her every now and then: "You are my companion, you are my companion."

They tell me, May, that I love people, and some reproach me for loving everybody. Yes, I love all people, I love them entirely without discrimination or preference, I love them as one unit, I love them because they are of God's spirit; but every heart has its special *Qiblah*,[1] every heart has a special direction towards which it turns when it is all alone. Every heart has a hermitage to which it retires by itself to seek comfort and consolation. Every heart yearns for another heart with which it may join in order to enjoy life's blessings and peace or forget life's pain [and suffering].

For years now I have felt that I have found the direction towards which my heart turns. And this feeling of mine has been a fact, simple, clear and beautiful. For this reason I rebelled against St Thomas, who visited me with doubts and queries. I will rebel against St Thomas and against his doubting hand in order that he may leave us alone in our heavenly seclusion, to enjoy our God-given faith.

It is a late hour of the night, and we have said very little indeed of what we wish to say. Perhaps it is better to speak in silence until morning. And in the morning my little loved one will stand by my side in front of our many works. And after that, when the day and its problems are over, we shall return to sit by the fire and talk.

And now bring your forehead nearer, like this—and may God bless you, and may God protect you.

Gibran

1 The direction towards which Muslims face at prayer (i.e. towards Mecca), metaphorically the goal or object of adoration.

New York Evening of Sunday, 2nd December (1923), Ten O'Clock.

Our day has been a hectically busy one. From nine in the morning till this hour we have been saying goodbye to people only to turn and greet more new arrivals. But all this while I have been glancing at my companion minute by minute, and have said to her: I thank and praise God, I thank and praise him, for we have met once more in our grove, and we each have in our pocket a loaf of bread instead of a book or a sketch-pad. I thank and praise God, for we have returned once more to herding our flock in the serene valley after a spell as schoolteachers. I thank and praise God because sweet Miriam[1] hears me in silence and understands my infatuation as I understand her compassion.

I have praised God and thanked the daytime and its duration because, for the space of this day, May has spoken with my tongue, she has given me her hand and so I have given her hand to others. All day long I have been seeing through her eyes, perceiving kindness in the faces of everyone, and listening with her ears, hearing sweetness in their voices.

You inquire after my health, and when you do so, my whole being is transformed into a mother full of compassion. I am in the best of health. The ailment I spoke of before has forsaken me, and has left me strong and in good spirits despite the grey streaks it has traced on the hair by my temples! The strange thing is that I cured myself unaided. I was practical and decisive, convinced that doctors are dreamers lost in the valleys of speculation and doubt. They were far more interested in studying "effects" and attempted to treat these with drugs; to "causes" they paid not the slightest heed. And as "the owner of the house who knows best what it holds", I went to the sea and the woods and spent six long months there without interruption, and in consequence all "causes" and "effects" vanished.

What do you say to our writing a book on modern medicine? Will you share its authorship with me?

We have now before us an important question we must discuss: you remember, of course, that a few weeks ago you revealed to me a very great "secret"; and you remember also that you did not reveal the "secret" until I had accepted your "conditions". What is strange is that I accepted the conditions before knowing what they were. What are these conditions? Please, dear lady, tell me what they are, I am ready to meet them all. You hesitated for a long time before revealing "your secret thoughts", so you have undoubtedly become anxious to unveil the conditions. What do you want, will you please tell me? What are the guarantees and terms you desire? Conditions are conditions, and he who is defeated must accept and honour them. The Ruhr problem[2] is problem enough for the world!

But I will not conceal from you the fact that after meeting your conditions I will investigate this dimple, or pseudo-dimple, that mocks my chin! Do you think I shall be lenient towards anything base in my chin which mocks the fine quality of the rest of it? Never!

I will cover this wicked dimple which does not respect its surroundings, "this dimple so distinguished in its intransigence and spitefulness". I will bury it in a long, thick beard; I will enshroud it in that part of my hair which has gone grey, and commit it to a coffin made of that part of my hair which has remained black. Indeed, I will wreak vengeance on this impudent dimple, which is unaware it cleaves to one whose anger touches off the anger in all beings and whose smile brings out the smile in them all.

Tomorrow we shall resume our discussion, but now let us go up onto the roof and stand awhile gazing at the stars of the night. Tell me, my little loved one, is the night more profound and wonderful than the heart of man? Are the galaxies more awe-inspiring and beautiful than what moves within the heart of man? Is there, in the night and stars, anything more sacred than that white flame flickering in God's hand?

[unsigned]

1 Another of Gibran's adaptations of May's name.

2 Ruhr, a river in Germany and also the industrial district, rich in metals and coal mines, that it crosses. This district was occupied by French and Belgian troops between 1923 and 1925, but was evacuated by recommendation of the Dawes Committee.

3rd (December 1923) at midnight (sic)

What can I say in response to your remarks about *The Prophet*? What should I say to you? This book is only a small part of what I have seen and of what I see every day, a small part only of the many things yearning for expression in the silent hearts of men and in their souls. There has never been anyone on the face of this earth with the ability to achieve anything by himself, as an individual completely cut off from all other human company. Nor is there anyone among us today who is able to do more than record what people say inadvertently. *The Prophet*, May, is only the first letter of a single word . . . In the past I was under the impression that this word was mine, in me and derived from me; for that reason I was unable to pronounce the first letter of that word. My inability to do so was the cause of my illness, indeed the cause of my soul's pain and suffering. After that God willed that my eyes be opened so that I could see the light, and God willed that my ears be opened so that I could hear other people pronounce this first letter, and God willed that I should open my lips and repeat that letter. I repeat it with joy and delight because for the first time I recognised that other people are everything and that I with my separate self am nothing. No-one knows better than you what freedom, comfort and tranquillity this realisation brought me, and no-one knows better than you about the feelings of someone who finds himself released from the prison of his own limited self.

And you, May, my grown-up little girl, will help me now to listen to the second letter in that word, and you will assist me in pronouncing it, and you will always remain with me.

Bring your forehead nearer, Miriam, bring it nearer, for there is a white rose in my heart which I wish to place on your forehead. How sweet love is when it stands trembling shyly before itself.

May God bless you. May God protect my little loved-one. May God fill her heart with the songs of angels.

Gibran

New York 31st December 1923

An envelope postmarked 31–12–23 contained a postcard of Mount Lafayette, New Hampshire, with the following message.

Last summer this valley reminded me of the valleys of North Lebanon.

No, no! I have never known a life more pleasant than one spent in valleys. I love the valleys in winter, Mary, when we sit by the fire, with the fragrance of burnt evergreen cypress filling the house and the snow falling outside, the wind blowing [it], the ice-lamps hanging outside the window-panes, and the distant sound of the river and the voice of the white storm uniting in our ears.

But if my little loved-one were not near me there would be no valley, no snow, no fragrance of cypress bough, no crystal lamps of ice, no river

song, no awe-inspiring storm . . . Let all these things vanish if my blessed little one be far away from them and from me.

And good night to that beloved pretty face.

Gibran

P.S. In the past I used to receive the newspaper cuttings from the newspaper cutting agency, but last year I stopped this. I became bored with newspapers then. In boredom there is something of spiritual drowsiness. So, forgive me, I'll try to get some cuttings again.

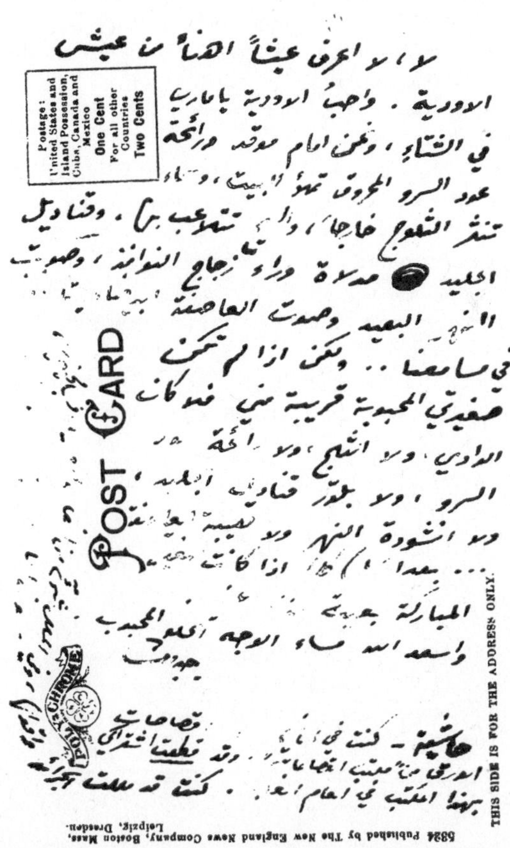

Boston 17th January 1924

An envelope postmarked 17–1–24 contained three Pierre de Chavannes postcards with the following message.

In the morning of my life I used to say de Chavannes[1] was the greatest French painter after Delacroix[2] and Carrière, but now that I have reached the afternoon of my life I would say de Chavannes is, without exception, the greatest painter of the nineteenth century, because, of all those painters, he had the simplest heart, the simplest thought, the simplest form of expression, and the purest of intentions. I would even go as far as to say that among painters he resembles Spinoza among philosophers.

When I was very young I used to visit the [Boston] Public Library and stand in awe before these paintings. Today I am in Boston once more and have visited the library; I stood before these same paintings with my beloved Miriam at my side, and I saw in them a beauty I have never seen in past years. But had my Miriam not been with me I would have seen nothing, for the eye without its light is but a cavity in the face, no more, no less.

Will you not bring your sweet forehead nearer? Like this—like this. May God shower his light upon that sweet forehead—Amen.

Gibran

1 Purvis (Pierre) de Chavannes (1824–1898), the French symbolist painter whose drawings were famous for their simplicity of colours and co-ordination of subjects.

2 Eugène Delacroix (1798–1863), the French painter who was considered the leader of the Romantic school of art.

continued

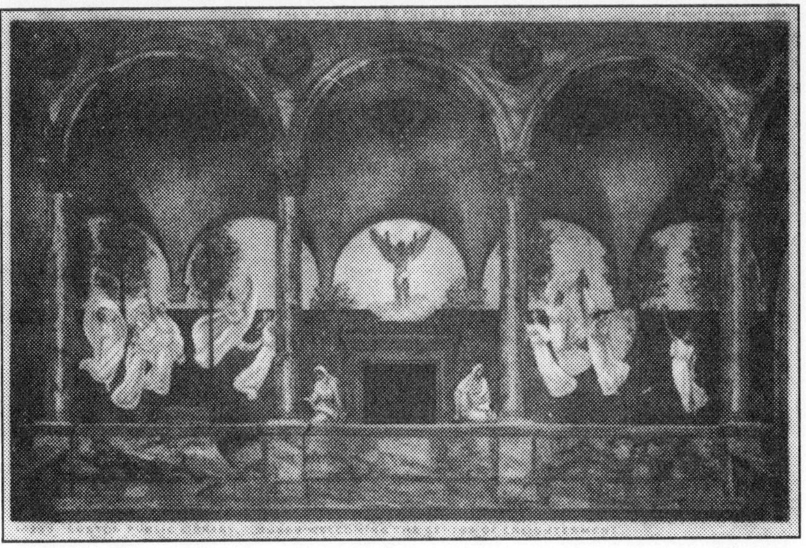

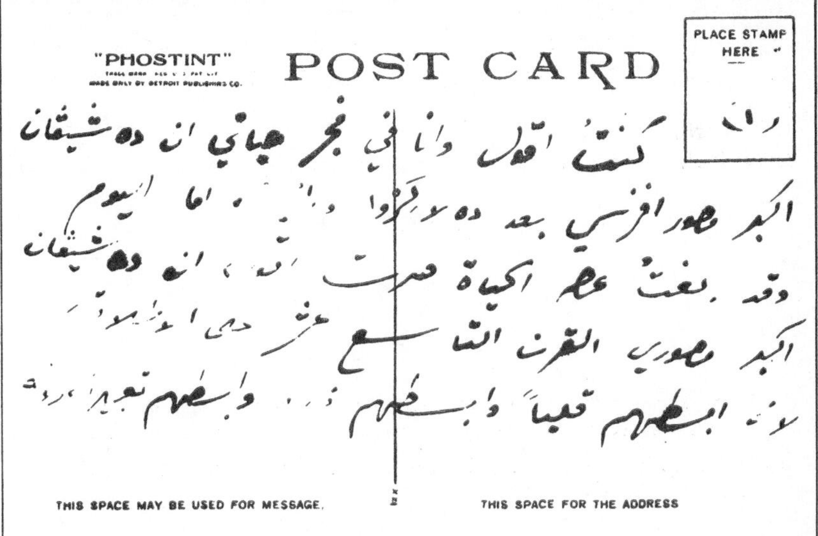
"PHOSTINT"
MADE ONLY BY DETROIT PUBLISHING CO.
POST CARD
PLACE STAMP HERE
THIS SPACE MAY BE USED FOR MESSAGE.
THIS SPACE FOR THE ADDRESS

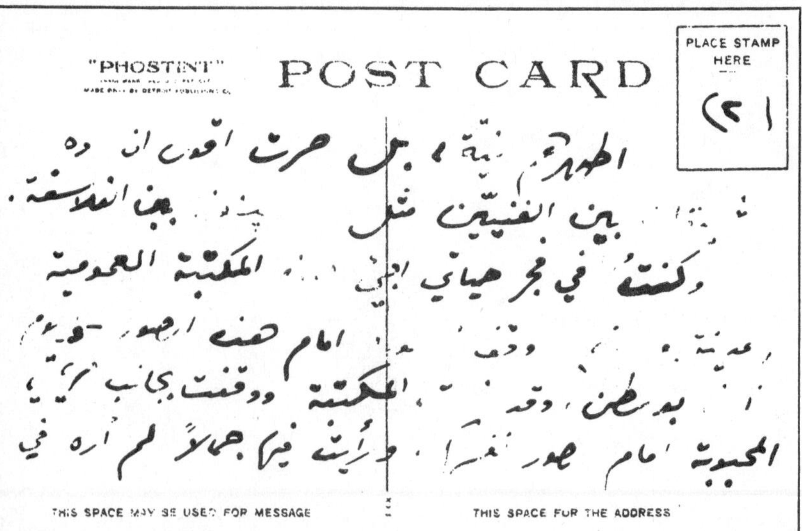

"PHOSTINT"

POST CARD

PLACE STAMP HERE

١ (٢)

الهدية [illegible] اجل حرت اقول ان ده

[illegible] بين الفنيتين مثل [illegible] بعض الفلاسفة.

وكنت في فجر حياتي [illegible] المكتبة العمومية

[illegible] امام صف [illegible]

[illegible] المكتبة ووقفت بجانب [illegible]

المحبوبة امام صور [illegible] ورأيت فيها جمالاً لم اره في

THIS SPACE MAY BE USED FOR MESSAGE

THIS SPACE FOR THE ADDRESS

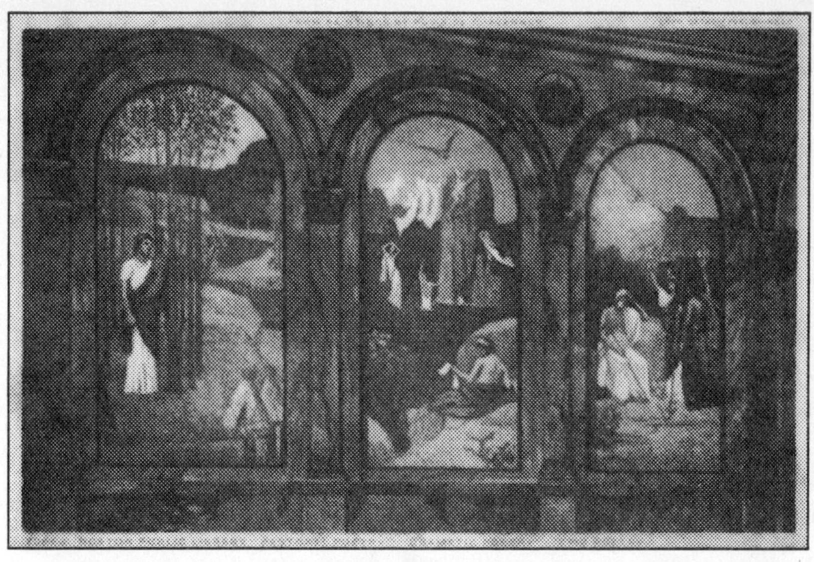

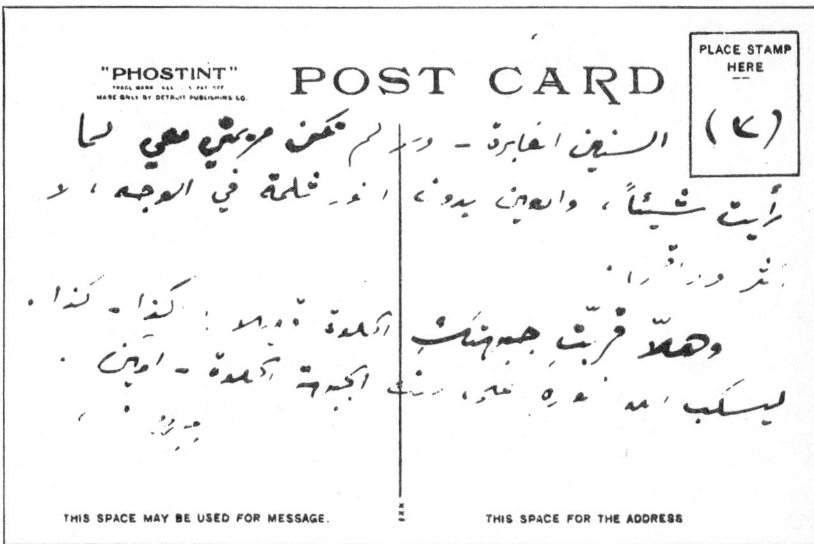
"PHOSTINT"
MADE ONLY BY DETROIT PUBLISHING CO.
POST CARD
PLACE STAMP HERE
THIS SPACE MAY BE USED FOR MESSAGE.
THIS SPACE FOR THE ADDRESS

New York 26th February 1924

Today we are experiencing a mighty snowstorm. Mary, you know how much I love all storms, especially snowstorms. I love snow, I love its whiteness, I love the fall of snow and its deep silence. I love snow in the heart of the distant unknown valleys where the snowflakes flicker in the light of the sun, twinkling awhile and then melting and quietly flowing away as they whisper their song.

I love snow and fire; both come from the same source, but my love for them has only ever been a form of readiness for a mightier love, more extensive and more sublime.

How well the words read:

> May, today we celebrate your birthday,
> And in you we celebrate life.

What a difference between this Arabic verse and that sent me recently by an American poet:

> Your honour and reward
> That you shall be crucified.

No matter. All that concerns me is to receive this honour and reward before the end comes.

Let us return to the subject of your "birthday". I wish to know on what day of the year my little loved one was born.[1] I want to know. I like birthdays and the celebration of birthdays. But Mary's birthday will assume top priority. You will tell me: "Every day is my birthday, Gibran", and I shall reply: "Yes, and I shall celebrate your birthday every single day, but there must be one special birthday once each year."

I am pleased you told me that my beard does not really belong to me. I am immensely pleased, and I think that the surrender of my beard is one of those conditions of international importance. This beard has occupied much of my thoughts and caused me unnecessary hardship. But now that my beard is the responsibility of someone other than myself, I shall spare it the touch of my hand and the edge of my razor. Let those who lay claim to it take upon themselves the responsibility for it. God bless those who claim ownership of it. Your percipience, however, relieves me of the task of elaborating on the technical side of the topiary in question . . .

SIC TRANSIT GLORIA MUNDI.[2]

. . . Consider, my sweet beloved, how jesting has led us to this Holiest of Holies in life. The [Arabic word] *rafiqah* ["companion"] caused my heart to flutter, so I stood up and began pacing the room as if in search of my "companion". What a strange effect certain words have on us sometimes—and how similar the sound of that word is to the peal of church-bells at sunset. It is the transmutation of that invisible inner self from mere utterance to silence, from mere action to worship.

You tell me that you fear love;[3] why, my little one? Do you fear the light of the sun? Do you fear the ebb and flow of the sea? Do you fear the dawning of the day? Do you fear the advent of spring? I wonder why you fear love?

I know that a mean-spirited love does not please you, just as I know a mean-spirited love does not please me. You and I are never satisfied with what is parsimonious in spirit. We want a great deal. We want everything. We want perfection. I say, Mary, that in this longing of ours lies the fulfilment; for if our will were one shadow of the many shadows of

God, we would undoubtedly attain one ray of light of the many lights of God for ourselves.

Oh, Mary, do not fear love; do not fear love, friend of my heart. We must surrender to it in spite of what it may bring in the way of pain, of desolation, of longing, and in spite of all the perplexity and bewilderment.

Listen, Mary: today I am in a prison of desires, desires which were born when I myself was born. And today I am fettered by the chains of an old idea, old as the seasons of the year. Can you then bear with me awhile, in my prison, so that we may eventually emerge into the light of the sun? Will you stand by me until the fetters are destroyed and we can walk freely and unhindered up to our mountain peak?

And now come nearer, bring your sweet forehead closer to me—like this, like this, and may God bless you and protect you, my heart's beloved companion.

Gibran

1 The letter was unwittingly written fifteen days after May's birthday (11th February).

2 "Thus passes the glory of the world".

3 See May Ziadah's letter (15th January 1924) quoted in the Introduction, pp. xvii.

New York 2nd November 1924

Mary,

You know the reason for your silence, but I do not. And it really is unjust for this state of incomprehension to be the source of the confusion that besets my days and nights.

Actions and words are all measured by the intentions and motives behind them, and my intention has been in the palm of God's hand. Tell me, my beloved little-one, what has become of you in the past year? Tell me, and may God reward you on my behalf.

May God protect you and fill your heart with His light.

Gibran

How sweet is my little beloved who remembers me daily in her prayers! How sweet she is, how great her heart and how beautiful her soul!

But how strange the silence of my little beloved, how strange her silence! This silence is as long as eternity, as deep as the dreams of the gods. It is a silence that cannot be translated into any mortal tongue. Do you not remember that when your turn came to write you did not do so? Have you forgotten that we had an agreement to embrace peace and concord before the night embraces the earth?

You inquire after my health and my thoughts, and after the matters that concern me. As to the question of how I am, I am exactly as you are, Mary. As for my thoughts, these are still enveloped in the mist, just as they have been whenever we have met—you and I—during the last thousand years. As for the matters that concern me nowadays, these are confused and disturbing but of the kind that a man like me must overcome whether he likes it or not.

Life, Miriam, is a beautiful song; some of us can only sound one note, while others can form a melodic line. And it seems to me, Miriam, that I can sound neither note nor melody. It seems to me that I am still in the mist that brought us together a thousand years ago.

Despite all this I am spending most of the time painting, and occasionally I escape to a faraway place in the countryside, carrying a small notebook in my pocket. Some day I shall send you a part of that notebook.

This is all I know about "I", so let us get back to what is important, let us get back to our sweet beloved. How are you, and how are your eyes? Are you as happy in Cairo as I am in New York? Do you pace about your room after midnight? Do you stand by your window and gaze every now and then at the stars? After that do you retire to your bed? And do you dry those smiles that melt in your eyes on the coverlet? Are you as happy in Cairo as I am in New York? I think of you, Mary, every day and every night. I think of you always, and in every thought there is a certain pleasure and a certain pain. What is strange, Miriam, is that whenever I think of you I secretly whisper to you: "Come and pour your troubles out here, here on my breast." And at times I call you by names unknown to anyone but loving fathers and compassionate mothers.

I kiss the palm of your right hand, and then kiss the palm of your left, beseeching God to protect and guard you, to fill your heart with His light and to keep you as the most beloved of all people.

Gibran

New York 12th January 1925

Mary,

On the sixth of this month I was thinking of you every minute and every second, and I was translating all that was said to me into the language of Mary and Gibran—a language which not one of the inhabitants of this earth can understand except Mary and Gibran . . . and you, of course, know that every day of the year is the birthday of each one of us.

The Americans are, of all peoples in the world, the most fond of celebrating birthdays and of sending and receiving birthday presents. And for a reason that has escaped me, the Americans shower their kindness on me on such occasions. On the sixth of this month I was embarrassed by their overwhelming kindness and filled with a deep sense of gratitude. But God knows the word I received from you was far dearer and more precious to me than anything and everything others can do for me. God knows that, and your heart knows it too.

After the celebrations we sat together, you and I, apart from the others and talked at length, saying to each other what cannot be spoken except by longing, and speaking what cannot be said except without hope. Then we gazed up at our distant star and were silent. After that we resumed our talk until the dawn of day, and your hand was placed on my throbbing heart until the morning broke.

May God watch over you and protect you, Miriam, and may He shower you with His light. May God keep you for him who loves you.

Gibran[1]

1 At the end of this letter Gibran drew the sketch of the hand below the flame that became the symbol of his love for May.

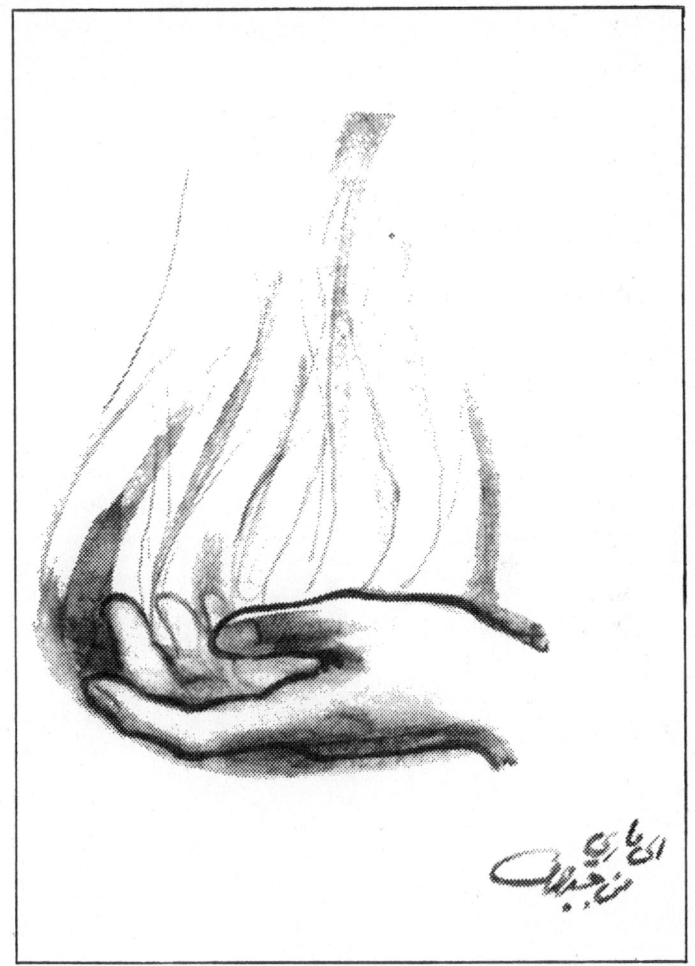

New York 6th February 1925

The following is the text of a note on a da Vinci postcard, enclosed in an envelope postmarked 6–2–25.

Mary,

I have never looked on any of Leonardo da Vinci's work without experiencing deep within myself the power of his charm, nor without the awareness that a part of his soul penetrates my own. I was a boy when I first came across the drawings of this incredible man. That was a moment I shall never forget as long as I live; and during that period of my life it acted for me like a compass needle for a ship lost in the mists of the sea.

I found this card among my papers today, and I thought I would send it to you to acquaint you with those things which plunged my youthful years into the valleys of gloom and loneliness and longing for the unknown. God protect you.

Gibran

continued

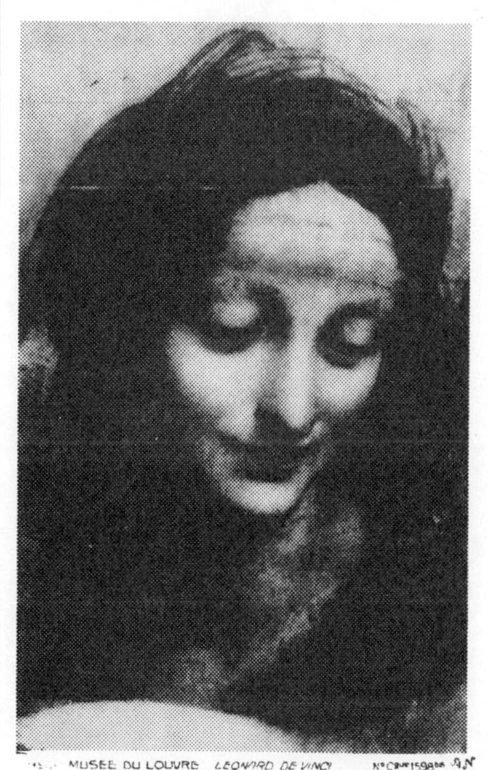

يا ماري. ما رأيت أثراً من آثار
ليوناردو دافنشي إلّا وشعرت
بقوة سحرية تتمشى في باطني [illegible]
[illegible]، بجزءٍ من روحانية تسرب
إلى روحي. كنتَ صبياً عندما
رأيت للمرة الأولى بعض رسوم هذا
الرجل العجيب. تلك ساعة سأذكرها

Made in France - Fabriqué en France

ما حييت فقد كانت من [illegible]
المغنطيسية من
الأيام بمقام الإبرة
سفينة تائهة في ضباب البحر
وجدت هذه البطاقة أمس
بين أوراقي فرأيت أن أبعث بها
إليك لتخبرك عن بعض تلك العواطف
التي كانت تسيّر شبابي في أودية الكآبة
والوحدة والشوق إلى ما لا أعرفه. الله يحرسك
جبران

New York 23rd March 1925

Mary,

That small file has caused you anxiety and annoyance. Forgive me. I thought I had sent it by the best and easiest route, but the opposite turned out to be the case. So forgive me, sweet friend, and heaven will reward you on my behalf.

So you have cut your hair. You have cut those black tresses with their beautiful waves. What am I to say to you? What am I to say when the scissors have forestalled all blame?

It doesn't matter! It doesn't matter! For I cannot contradict the advice you were given by the Italian hairdresser . . . May God have mercy on the souls of the fathers of all Italians.

Not content with informing me of that tremendous loss, my dear friend desired to add insult to injury by addressing [me as] "a poet and artist who is enamoured by elegant fair hair, for he derives pleasure from nothing but fair hair, sings the praises of nothing but fair hair, and cannot abide the existence of anything but heads of fair hair".

Oh Lord, my God, forgive Mary every word she has uttered, pardon her, and wash away her mistakes with the effulgence of your divine light. Reveal unto her, in her dreams and in her waking, the utter "catholicism" of Your servant Gibran in any matter related to beauty. Oh God, send one of Your angels to inform her that this servant of Yours dwells in a hermitage with many windows, through which he is able to observe the manifestations of Your beauty and excellence in all things and in all places; and that he sings the praises of dark hair as much as he does of fair hair, and that, indeed, he marvels just as much over black eyes as he does over blue eyes. I

beseech you, my Lord and my God, to exhort
Mary not to humiliate poets and artists in the
person of Your servant Gibran . . . Amen.

After this long prayer, how can you expect me to discuss the demerits of natural beards? Absolutely not! However, I will look for an Italian hairdresser in this city, and ask him whether he is able to transform an untrimmed, natural beard into a simple rounded beard—round, that is, by means of a geometrical compass! Since I am an authority in surgical matters, I am not afraid of an operation.

But let us return to the discussion about your eyes.

How are your eyes, Mary? You know, you know in your heart that the health of your eyes concerns me very greatly. How can you question this when it is with your eyes that you see what is hidden behind the veil? You know that the human heart is governed by the laws of distance and measurement, and that the strongest and most deep-seated feeling in our hearts is that to which we surrender, and in surrendering to it we feel a pleasure and a comfort and a tranquillity notwithstanding our inability to explain or analyse its nature. It is sufficient that this feeling is profound, strong and divine. So why do you question and doubt? Which one of us, Mary is able to translate the language of the invisible world into that of the visible? Which one of us can say: "In my soul burns a white flame, and such and such are its causes, or such and such is its meaning, and such and such will be its effects"?

I have asked after your eyes, Mary, because I am greatly concerned about your eyes, because I love their light; I love their distant gaze; and I love the dancing images of their dreamy looks.

But my concern for your eyes in no way suggests that I am any the less concerned for your forehead or your fingers.

May God bless you, beloved Mary, and may He bless your eyes, your forehead, your fingers, and may He always keep you for me.

Gibran

Boston 28th March 1925

The following is the text of a note on a Mantegna postcard, enclosed in an envelope postmarked 28–3–25.

Mary,

I have great admiration for Mantegna,[1] and in my opinion every painting by him is a beautiful lyric poem. But you must visit Florence, Venice and Paris to see the works of this man for yourself, strange and eccentric works, with at least as much inspiration as oddness in them.

Good night to the pretty face.

Gibran

1 Andrea Mantegna (1431–1506), the Italian painter who was one of the pioneers of Italian Renaissance Art.

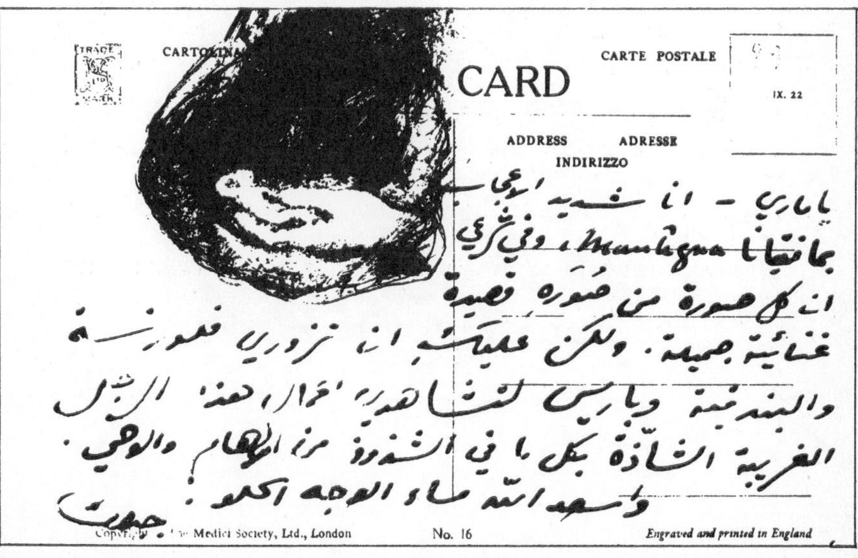

CARTE POSTALE

CARD

IX. 22

ADDRESS ADRESSE

INDIRIZZO

يا ماري – انا شديد الاعجاب

بمانتينيا Mantegna، وفي رأيي

ان كل صورة من صوره قصيدة

غنائية جميلة. ولكن عليك ان تزوري فلورنسة

والبندقية وباريس لتشاهدي آثار هذا الرجل

الغريبة الشاذة بكل ما في الشذوذ من الالهام والوحي.

واسعد الله مساء الوجه الحلو!

جبران

Copyright ... Medici Society, Ltd., London No. 16 *Engraved and printed in England*

New York 30th March 1925

Mary,

Yes, my four-week silence was due to Spanish Fever—no more, no less.

I find it very difficult—extremely difficult, in fact—to complain of any ailment that touches me. When I am taken ill I have only one desire, and that is not to be seen by others, even by those whom I love and who love me. In my opinion the best cure for any malady is complete seclusion.

However, I am well now, perhaps better than merely "well", and I can scarcely conceal my secret feeling that my health is "behemothian" ["fighting-fit"] This is how a tough-guy from Bisharri used to describe his health when asked how he was.[1]

The special issue of *al-Sa'ih*[2] appeared late, as usual. On the 'phone this morning I spoke with the owner/editor, who told me that he has been and is still sending you copies of his paper, whether or not they are special issue.

It is indeed a great exaggeration for you, sweet Miriam, to say that the editor of *al-Sa'ih* was annoyed at you because you did not send him an article for his paper's special issue. How can you think that anyone could be annoyed at you with me around here in New York? I have said it a thousand times: "We artists are not literary manufactories, we are not machines you feed at one end with ink and paper and expect to produce articles and poems at the other. We write when we wish to write, not when you want us to. So do us a favour and leave us alone, for we belong to one world and you to another, you are not one of us and we are not of your kind." What do you say to this strict tone of mine? But seriously, though—joking apart—haven't you noticed that most newspaper and magazine proprietors think the writer is like a phonograph because they themselves were born with phonographic ideas?

Here in New York we are at the beginning of spring, and there is an awakening and an enchantment in the air; the spirit is full of youth and the light of daybreak; trips to the countryside are very much like the visits made by the priest and priestesses of Astarte and Adonis to the cave of Afqa.[3]

In a few days Jesus will rise from the dead to bestow life on those buried under the earth's surface; apple- and almond-trees will blossom, and melodious song will return to the rivers and streams.

You will be with me on every one of the days of April, and you will remain with me after April—every day and every night.

May God protect you and keep you, beloved Miriam.

Gibran

1 The Arabic original is "Bahmouttia", derived from the Hebrew word "b'hemoth". The English word "behemoth" means "enormous creature", and is itself derived from the Hebrew word.

2 *Al-Sa'ih* (*The Tourist*), the Arab immigrants' newspaper founded in New York by the poet Abdel Massih Haddad in 1912. Its last issue was published in 1957.

3 Afqa, a village in the north of Lebanon, rich in ruins, especially the ruins of the temple of Adonis and Astarte. It also contains a cave from which originate the springs of the river Ibrahim.

New York (?) May 1927[1]

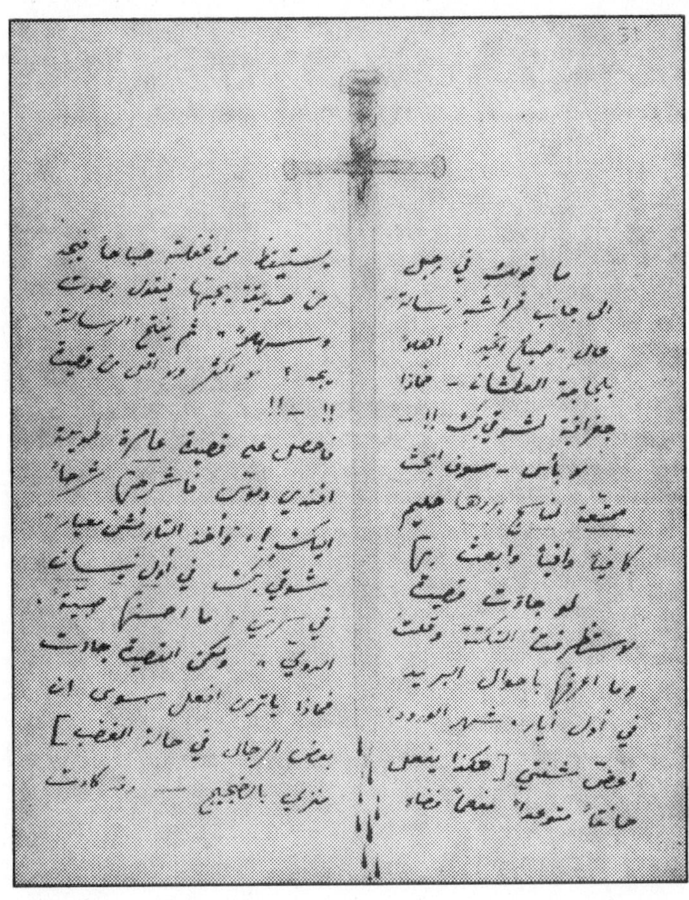

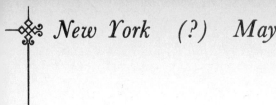

What can you say about a man who, when he wakes in the morning to find by his bedside a letter from a friend he loves, cries in a loud voice, "Good morning; welcome!"; and then, when he opens the letter with all the impatience of a thirsty man who has found a water-bottle; he finds no more and no less than a poem on geography by Shawqi Bey?[2]

No matter, I shall find out a long, elaborate and entertaining poem by Haleem Effendi Dammoos[3] and then write a fully detailed analysis of it and send it to you.

If Shawqi's poem had arrived on 1 April I should have appreciated the joke, and would have thought to myself: "What a terrific girl she is, and how well she knows the international mail service." But the poem arrived on the first day of May, the month of roses, so what was I to do but bite my lip in fury (this being what some men do when they are angry), burst out in rage, shouting threats and filling my house with noise.

Indeed I shall study the wisdom in the words: "An eye for an eye and a tooth for a tooth", and I will send you all that the muse has inspired in the poets-laureate of Arabic verse.

I ask you now: "How am I to spend the rest of this day before I forgive you?" The poem of your poet-laureate has filled my mouth with dust, and I must wash away the taste with twenty cups of coffee and twenty cigarettes; not only that, but I must also read twenty poems by Keats,[4] Shelley[5] and Blake,[6] and a poem by Majnun Layla.[7]

In spite of everything open the palm of your hand . . . like this . . . as people do . . .

Gibran

1 The date of issue on the envelope of this letter is unclear.

2 Ahmed Shawqi (1869–1932), Egypt's poet-laureate of the day and one of the major Arab poets of the early twentieth century. "Beck" or "Bey" was an honorific title of Turkish origin, used in Egypt until 1952, the date of the Egyptian revolution, when all titles were abrogated.

3 Haleem Dammoos, a Lebanese poet who lived in the first half of the twentieth century, famous as a poet of occasions.

4 John Keats (1795–1821), the poet, about whom Gibran wrote a poem entitled "Bihurouf min Nar" ("With Letters of Fire").

5 Percy Bysshe Shelley (1792–1822), the poet, was mentioned repeatedly in Gibran's letters to Mary Haskell.

6 William Blake (1757–1822), the poet and illustrator, was one of the most important influences on Gibran's tastes in literature and art. Gibran borrowed the title of one of his books, *A Tear and A Smile*, from Blake.

7 Majnun Layla is a seventh-century semi-mythical poet whose original name is said to have been Qays ibn al-Mulawwah (d. AD 688). According to legend, Qays became infatuated to the point of madness (hence the legendary name he has assumed—Majnun) with a woman of his own tribe named Layla, who reciprocated his love but was, against her will, wedded to another man at the behest of her father. As a legendary character and love poet *par excellence* in Arab folk-tradition, he appears as the hero of innumerable Arabic, Persian and Turkish romances extolling the power of eternal love.

New York 10th December 1929

Mary, my dear friend,

I learnt today that your father has travelled beyond the golden horizon and has reached that goal towards which we all make our pilgrimage. What am I to say to you? Mary, you are far too sublime in thought and in your choice of the words you wish to hear for the soothing platitudes of consolation. But in my heart there is a strong desire to stand before you, and a longing to hold your hand in mine in silence, feeling all that fills your soul, inasmuch as he who is near to you and yet still a stranger is able to share in what you feel.

May God bless you, Mary, and may He protect you every day and every night; and may God keep you for your friend.

Gibran

New York 17th December 1930

Form No. 6B.

WESTERN UNION CABLEGRAM

THE WESTERN UNION TELEGRAPH COMPANY. ANGLO-AMERICAN TELEGRAPH Co. LD.

RECEIVED AT 22, GREAT WINCHESTER STREET, LONDON, E.C.2. (Tel. No. London Wall 0800.)

TAY2PZ 1355
NEWYORK 39

5 DEC 17 AM 3 06

CLT POST
MARIE ZIADAH
1 ELOUI PACHA ST
CAIRO....LONDON.

WAS AWAY THEN RECEIVED GRACIOUS AND SWEET LETTER CANNOT WRITE WITH SICK HAND THIS MESSAGE IS OF AFFECTION AND GOOD WISHES FOR HAPPY CHRISTMAS AND SINGING NEW YEAR

GIBRAN

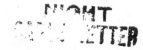

No inquiry respecting this Message can be attended to without the production of this paper.

Khalil Gibran

جبران خليل جبران

The Life of Kahlil Gibran: a chronology

1883 Gibran was born on January 6 near the Holy Cedar Grove on the edge of Wadi Qadisha (The Holy or Sacred Valley) in the town of Bisharri, Lebanon. His mother Kamileh, the daughter of a clergyman, named Istiphan Rahmeh, was a widow when she married Khalil Gibran, father of the poet. Kamileh's first husband was Hanna Abd-es-Salaam Rahmeh, by whom she had one son, Boutros, who was six years old when Gibran was born.

1885 Miriana, Gibran's first sister, was born.

1887 Sultanah, Gibran's second sister, was born.

1895 Kahlil, his half-brother Boutros, his mother, and his two sisters emigrated to the United States, settling in Boston's Chinatown, while his father remained in Lebanon.

1897 Gibran returned to Lebanon, where he began a course of intensive study at al-Hikmah School. He studied a wide variety of subjects beyond those prescribed in the curriculum, and immersed himself in Arabic literature, ancient and modern. He also familiarized himself with contemporary literary movements in the Arab world.

1899 During the summer vacation at Bisharri, Gibran fell desperately in love with a beautiful young woman. Although there is much conjecture as to the nature of his relationship and the identity of the young woman, it is certain that Gibran found his first love-affair both frustrating and disappointing. In the autumn he returned to Boston by way of Paris, and several years later described the unhappy affair in *The Broken Wings*.

1902 Gibran returned to Lebanon once more, this time as a guide and interpreter to an American family, but was forced to hurry back to Boston on hearing of the death of his sister, Sultanah, and of the serious illness of his mother.

1903 In March his half-brother Boutros died, and his mother died in June, leaving Gibran and his sister Miriana in Boston. His mother, half-brother, and younger sister all died of tuberculosis.

1904 By now Gibran was beginning to attract attention as an artist. Fred Holland Day, a well-known photographer, became Gibran's first patron, holding at his studio in January an exhibition of the poet's paintings and drawings. In February a second exhibition was held at the Cambridge School, a private educational institution owned and operated by Mary Haskell, who became Gibran's close friend, patroness and benefactress.
At the Cambridge School he also met a beautiful and impulsive young woman of French origin, Emilie Michel, who was known to all her acquaintances as Micheline and with whom, it is said, Gibran fell in love.

1905 Gibran published *al-Musiqah* (*Music*), his first book in Arabic.

1906 Gibran published a savage attack against the Church and the State in *'Ara' is al-Muruj* (*Nymphs of the Valley*), which earned him the reputation of being a rebel and a revolutionary, a reputation which the publication of his later mystical works only partially mitigated.

1908 Besides arranging for the publication of *al-Arwah al-Mutamarridah* (*Spirits Rebellious*), Gibran also worked on *Falsafat al-Din wa'l-Tadayyun* (*The Philosophy of Religion and Religiosity*), which was never published.

Through the generosity of Mary Haskell, who was determined to help Gibran fulfil his ambition to become a great artist and thinker, he went to Paris, visiting London on the way, to study art at the Academie Julien and at the Ecoles des Beaux-Arts.
During his stay in Paris he came into contact with European literature, read the works of contemporary English and French writers. He also became especially interested in the work of William Blake, who greatly influenced his thought and art; and for a while fell under the spell of Friedrich Nietzsche's *Thus Spake Zarathustra*; but Nietzsche's influence, unlike that of Blake was short-lived.

1909 Gibran continued his studies in Paris, where he met again an old classmate from al-Hikmah, Yusuf al-Huwayik, also an art student. The two men became close friends, and together tried to acquaint themselves with modern trends in painting. They found, however, that they had little sympathy with Cubism, which one of them described as a "lunatic revolution", and instead reaffirmed their loyalty to the classical tradition. They also met the sculptor Auguste Rodin, and although this meeting lasted only for a few seconds, Rodin was to exert a powerful influence on Gibran's art. His teacher in Paris was in fact Maitre Lawrence, whose art Gibran so detested that eventually he left him and began to work on his own.
Gibran's father died in Lebanon.

1910 Gibran, Ameen Rihani, and Yusuf al-Huwayik met in London and laid many plans for a cultural renaissance of the Arab world. Among these plans was one for the founding of an opera house in Beirut, the outstanding feature of which was to be two domes symbolizing the reconciliation between Christianity and Islam.
After his return to Boston in October, Gibran proposed marriage to Mary Haskell, who was ten years his senior, but he was not accepted.

1911 At a time of intense political activity occasioned by the freeing of Arab territories from Ottoman rule, Gibran founded *'al-Halga' l-Dhahabiyyah* (*The Golden Circle*), one of many semi-political Arab societies which sprang up in Syria, Lebanon, Constantinople, Paris and New York. But the Golden Circle was not popular among Arab immigrants and was dissolved after the first meeting.
Gibran began to earn his living through portrait painting.

1912 Gibran moved from Boston to New York, where he hired a studio at 51 West Tenth Street, between Fifth and Sixth Avenue. "The Hermitage", as Gibran called his studio, remained his home until his death. He published *al-Ajnihah 'l-Mutakassirah* (*The Broken Wings*), his autobiographical narrative, on which he had been working since 1903.
A literary and love relationship began between Gibran and May Ziadah, a Lebanese writer living in Egypt. Although they knew each other only through their correspondence, which lasted for more than twenty years, they achieved a rare intimacy and harmony of understanding which was broken only by Gibran's death.

1914 Gibran collected a number of his prose poems which had appeared in different magazines since 1904, and published them under the titles *Dam'ah wa'Ibtisamah (A Tear and a Smile)*. In December an exhibition of his paintings and drawings was held at the Montross Galleries, New York.

1917 Two other exhibitions of Gibran's works were held: one at the Knoedler Galleries, New York; the other at the Doll and Richards Galleries, Boston.

1918 Gibran published *The Madman*, his first book written in English.

1919 Gibran published *Twenty Drawings*, a collection of his drawings with an introduction by Alice Raphael, and also *al-Mawakib* (*The Procession*), a philosophical poem illustrated by Gibran himself and containing some of his best drawings.

1920 In addition to publishing *al-'Awasif* (*The Tempests*), a collection of short narratives and prose poems which had appeared in various journals between 1912 and 1918, and his second English book, *The Forerunner*, Gibran became founder-president of a literary society called *al-Rabita 'l-Qalamiyya (Arrabitah)*. This society, which included among its members such distinguished Arab immigrants as 'Abd-al-Masih Haddad, Naseeb 'Arida, Mikhail Naimy, Rashied Ayyub, Nadra Haddad, William Catzflis, Iliya Abu Madi and Wadi' Bahut, exerted a powerful influence on the work of immigrant Arab poets (Shu'ara' 'l-Mahjar) and on successive generations of Arab writers.

1921 Gibran published a thematic "play", *Iram Dhat al-Imad (Iram, City of Lofty Pillars)*, written in Arabic and taking the form of a discourse on mysticism.
His health began to deteriorate.

1922 In January another exhibition of his work was held in Boston, this time at the Women's City Club.

1923 Gibran published *al-Badayi' wa'l-Tarayif (Beautiful and Rare Sayings)* in which he included his own sketches (drawn from imagination when he was seventeen) of some of the greatest Arab philosophers and poets such as Ibn Sina (Avicenna), Al Ghazzali, al-Khansa', Ibn al-Farid, Abu Nuwas, Ibn al-Mugafa' and others.
He published *The Prophet*, his most successful work.

1926 Gibran published *Sand and Foam*, a book of aphorisms some of which were first written in Arabic and then translated into English.

1928 Gibran published *Jesus, the Son of Man*, his longest work.

1931 Two weeks before his death, he published *The Earth Gods*. Gibran died on Friday, April 10, at St. Vincent's Hospital, New York, after a long and painful illness, described in the autopsy as "cirrhosis of the liver with incipient tuberculosis in one of the lungs." His body lay in a funeral parlor for two days and thousands of admirers came to pay their last respects. It was then taken to Boston, where a funeral service was conducted in the Church of our Lady of the Cedars. The body was then taken to a vault to await its return to Lebanon, where it arrived at the port of Beirut on August 21. After a magnificent reception unique in the history of Lebanon, Gibran's body was carried to Bisharri to its final resting place in the old chapel of the Monastery of Mar Sarkis. Not far from Mar Sarkis a permanent Gibran museum has been established by the people of Bisharri with the sponsorship and encouragement of the Government of Lebanon.
At his death, Gibran left two works which were published posthumously: the completed *Wanderer*, which appeared in 1932; and the unfinished *Garden of the Prophet*, which was completed and published in 1933 by Barbara Young, an American poetess who claimed to have been Gibran's companion during the last seven years of his life.

*All dates are as accurate as is possible, given the lack of documentation for a number of the events listed here: it was only with the discovery of these letters for instance that so central a date as that of Gibran's birth was verified as falling on 6 January 1883, rather than on 6 December of the same year. Other dates will no doubt undergo the same process of revision as new information on the author come to light.

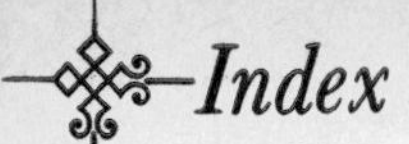

Index

Note: The abbreviation G in index stands for Kahlil Gibran
Figures in italics refer to illustrations on the page cited.